Archery Handbook

BY EDMUND H. BURKE

New York

Published by ARCO PUBLISHING COMPANY, Inc.
219 Park Avenue South, New York, N.Y. 10003

Copyright © Fawcett Publications, Inc., 1954

All Rights Reserved

Third Printing 1965

Library of Congress Catalog Card Number:54-9236

Arco Catalog Number: 842

Printed in the United States of America

Unless otherwise credited, photos throughout this book were made by its author

Contents

ARCHERY HANDBOOK

Archery Through The Ages	4
Selection Of Equipment	18
Bow Making	24
How To Make Bowstrings	40
Arrows And Arrow Making	50
Equipment Cost And Bow Breakdown	64
How To Use Equipment	68
Archery Lesson In Photos	84
Hunting And Seasons	98
Practice And Games	122
Accessories	134
Glossary Of Terms	142

Photo by courtesy of Centaur Archery Co.

ARCHERY THROUGH THE AGES

One of the three basic discoveries that led mankind out of the caves and into civilization, archery is older than recorded history, yet an ultra-modern sport.

Photo by Anthony Lane
Courtesy Paul Bunyan Bait Co.

Archery Through the Ages

Unless otherwise noted, all drawings and photos in this chapter are by courtesy of The American Museum of Natural History or by the author, who copied them.

NO one knows who made the first bow and arrow. Somewhere back in the vast dimness of time one of our ancestors tied a piece of leather thong to the opposite ends of a stick, fitted another smaller stick onto the thong—and the first archer came into being. Modern archeologists, working to reconstruct the picture of those days for us, feel safe in saying that certain tribes of the Neanderthal race used the bow over one hundred thousand years ago. Considering that our recorded history covers the short span of approximately five thousand years, the bow is certainly part of man's oldest inheritance. When the later Cro-Magnon man appeared on the scene, after the Ice Ages, he was well equipped with bows and arrows. His magnificent cave paintings gave us a colorful and accurate look at hunting in those days. Here on our own continent, the Folsom man, who roamed through the southwest twenty-five thousand years ago, was a good archer. The proof of his accuracy is to be seen today in the arrowheads imbedded in the ribs of a now extinct buffalo.

Actually the date of archery's invention is comparatively unimportant. What really counts is the fact that the use of the bow is

Small drawings throughout chapter are reproductions of cave paintings from prehistoric times, found in Alpera, Spain

In Ancient India archery symbolized food: mythic god holds corn-sheaf bow, blossoming arrow.

In Ancient Egypt, the military made use of bowmen: soldier's uniform allowed arm freedom.

The early savages of Africa were bow hunters, although the aboriginal tribes of Australia had no bows.

without question one of the big factors that gave man the place he occupies in today's world. It may seem difficult to see how man, with his long range bombers and their cargoes of atomic power, can owe anything to the simple bow and arrow. Yet it was this same bow and arrow which helped to raise man above the rest of the animal kingdom, which set him on the path of progress. The staid Encyclopedia Brittanica ranks the discovery of archery as one of the three most important cultural advances in the history of mankind—equalled only by the discovery of fire and the development of speech. Other authorities rank archery with fire and the wheel. Without speech man was only an animal, unable to communicate with facility; without fire, he remained an animal; but without the bow man might not have survived at all. In comparison with the other members of the animal kingdom, man is an incredible weakling. Given the bow he became their superior—able to protect himself and able to feed himself, all in comparative safety. It was more than a weapon.

Without realizing it, man was using stored energy when he used his bow. Some of the greatest problems that man has faced and is facing, have to do with the holding of energy. The bow was the first instance where he met and solved the problem; for no matter how briefly, man holds stored energy in his hands when the bow is at full draw. In reaching full draw the energy is gradually gathered, stored temporarily, and then released in a fraction of a second.

When the bow came into being it was widely distributed. Apparently no one nation or tribe can ever claim sole credit for its invention. The Israelites, according to the Bible, were great archers, as were their oppressors the Egyptians. The Babylonians, Assyrians, Persians, Greeks, Chinese and Japanese were all nations favoring archery. In Rome the bow was not highly developed until late in the time of the Caesars when mounted bowmen became a vital part of the Roman legions. Only in Australia was the bow missing. Australia was in its Stone

ARCHERY THROUGH THE AGES

In the jungles of South America, archery has been known for centuries: even today huge Pan-American airliners are showered with arrows.

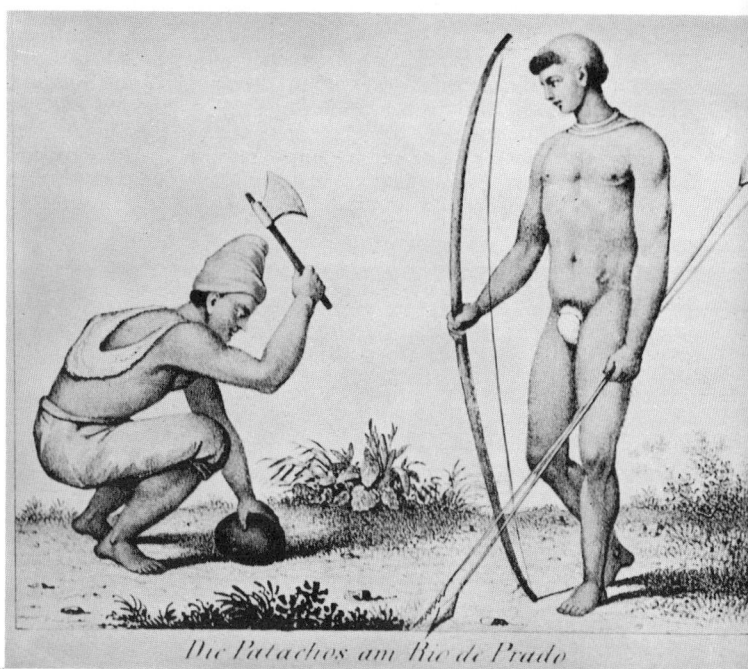

Natives of Ceylon, shown at left, are called Veddas: these nomad hunters use long bows with long spear-like arrows.

African natives also use extra long arrows, resembling spears, even with a double-barbed head: bows are long also.

Age when white men first landed there. Whether or not, in the course of cultural development, the aborigine would have developed a bow we'll never know, so it seems a little unfair to draw a correlation between the backwardness of the natives and the lack of archery. But the facts remain, and we may draw our own conclusions.

The bow and its accompanying sheaf of arrows was man's constant companion for centuries. It fell into disuse gradually, supplanted by gunpowder, the crossbow and inertia. Men found it easier to aim a gun, no matter how slow firing, instead of spending the necessary hours of practice with a bow. By 1600 the bow was past its prime, at least as far as the West was concerned, but great sections of the globe continued its use as they still do. Even today, planes flying over certain sections of South America are showered with arrows, driven into the air by Indian archers. And when our country was in its infancy, Benjamin Franklin seriously advised our Continental Army to remember the archer's weapons, saying, "they are good weapons, not easily cast aside."

But our concern is not with the history or past performance of the bow and arrow. We're interested in what archery is today

The early Huns that overran Europe during the Fifth and Sixth Centuries brought cruel clubs and archery with them.

ARCHERY THROUGH THE AGES

Early Arabians used short but powerful bows that resembled very much the modern recurve bow.

Scottish tribes before the Middle Ages used bow and arrow for warfare and hunting.

Note the strange axe-blade-harpoon shape of arrow-point of shaft held by early Esquimeau who fished and hunted seal by archery.

A Tschutiskian with his wife and child is shown here in full armour: his weapons are a recurve bow and a long spear. He roamed sands of Mongolia.

—America's fastest growing sport. When archery was displaced by gunpowder as a weapon, it became a sport and an art. As such it is certainly one of the oldest in the world ranking with music, painting and the dance.

The history of archery in the United States goes back to 1828, when a group of young men founded the United Bowmen of Philadelphia, and to that organization—still strongly active—America owes its modern interest in archery. The sport went through a series of ups and downs for nearly a century. A solid core of archers kept it alive through wars and depressions, but it remained for the exploits of Dr. Saxton Pope—who killed seventeen African lions with a long bow—to really ignite the imagination of the American public.

We've always been a nation of hunters, both by inheritance and by inclination. And while few of us are averse to hunting with a gun, even the most avid rifleman will admit an ungrudging respect for a man who faces a full grown charging lion with only a long bow and the "cloth yard shaft" for protection. Today we're privileged in having another great hunting archer—Howard Hill—whose exploits have also converted many a new devotee.

A large part, then, of archery's current phenomenal growth is due to hunting. And bow hunting is a self-perpetuating and self-promoting sport. It's an established fact that our most ardent sportsmen are also our most ardent conservationists When they realized that bow hunting was not only a true test of stamina, courage and woodsmanship but an excellent conservation method as well, hunting archers were born by the thousands. As more and more states began to recognize the bow hunter by the institution of special bow seasons and setting up bow hunting areas, more and more archers took up the sport until forty-six of the forty-eight states now have special provisions for archery.

A second factor in archery's growth is the universal appeal of the sport. Women may not pull as heavy bows as their mates but that hasn't stopped them from knocking down just as much game, or scoring just as high on the targets. In fact archery is an ideal family sport, one in which every

ARCHERY THROUGH THE AGES

Archer and crossbowmen meet symbolically in the year 1250 A.D. The longbow would soon be passe.

An archer of France during the Thirteenth Century used a short powerful bow, carried arrows in belt.

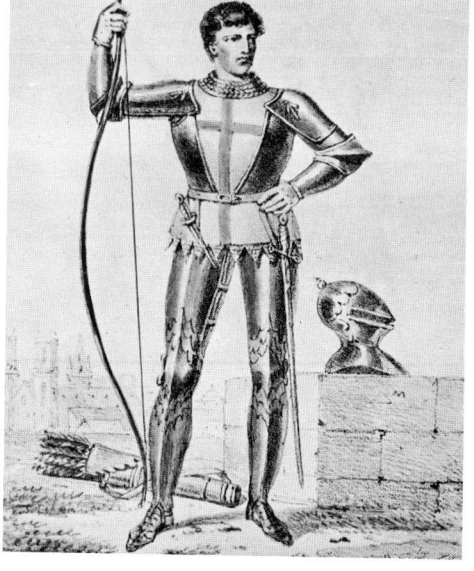

Although crossbow soon would replace longbow across Channel, Paris military still used it in 1470.

member can participate and compete. Age is no bar in archery. In the 1953 National Archery Association Tournament men in their eighties stood on the line, shooting high scores, while a hundred yards away teen-agers tried to keep up with their elders.

With the increased interest in archery came some surprising developments in equipment. Just as the past two or three decades brought thousands of new fans into the game, they have also brought changes in ideas, design and materials. Basically archery had remained unchanged for at least five thousand years. But as more and more people from every walk of life took up archery, they brought to it broader thinking, new ideas, new techniques. Many of the ideas and techniques were tried and abandoned—because they weren't serviceable—but others have become part and

In the reign of King Edward IV, the English longbow was yet in evidence among Royal Guardsmen.

Soldiers of the Turkish Navy in Seventeeth Century were equipped with a sabre and a longbow.

ARCHERY THROUGH THE AGES

By the end of Eighteenth Century, however, archery had become a sport, one in which even the ladies had a hand. This drawing from the early Nineteenth Century was intended as a fashion plate to advertise new dress styles, but it also shows growing popularity of archery sport.

More recent Mongolian warrior of last century still used bow and arrow for hunting and war.

Compare women tournament archers of today in loose comfortable clothing with girls shown above.

Traditional Japanese bow has hand-grip located far below center, yet is accurate.

French artist's conception of Amazon, left, shows her in act of drawing shaft.

Chinese Mandarin poses elegantly with bow, quiver of arrows, and cutlass sword.

parcel of today's archery. Engineer-archers and archer-physicists brought to the sport their own wealth of background, for practical application. Their theories, ideas and designs were taken in turn by archer-chemists and archer-machinists, with an end result that far surpasses anything in the whole long history of the sport. Today's bows and arrows are designed and built according to the best conceivable patterns, with the net result that American archers and their equipment are second to none in the world.

One of the nice things about archery is that, in spite of its terrific advances, it remains an inexpensive hobby. It is possible to spend a sizable amount on equipment, but it certainly isn't necessary. The novice can still make good tackle—using the new designs and the new materials—and the advanced archer sometimes gets his biggest thrill in using equipment he's made himself. It inspires pride.

Today's archer is a far cry from the stout English bowman at Agincourt. That staunch veteran—and to him great praise is due—would still know that a bow was a

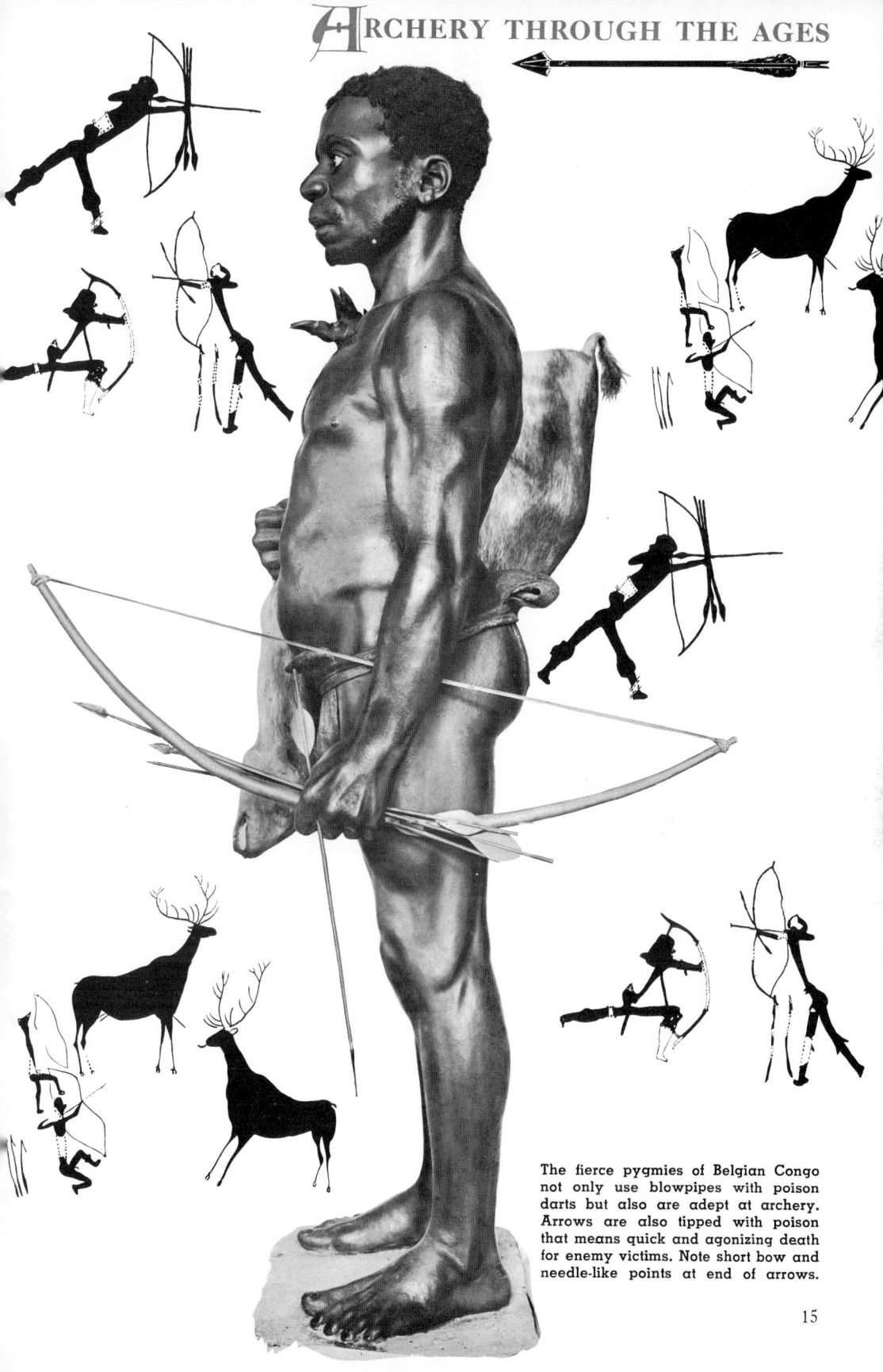

Archery Through the Ages

The fierce pygmies of Belgian Congo not only use blowpipes with poison darts but also are adept at archery. Arrows are also tipped with poison that means quick and agonizing death for enemy victims. Note short bow and needle-like points at end of arrows.

Infants barely able to walk are trained in the art of archery by contemporary African natives.

The American Indian shown on facing page was not a very good archer but was still good hunter.

Below is another American Indian: skill at tracking game to get close made up for bad bowing.

Archery Through the Ages

bow and an arrow an arrow. But close examination of their composition would convince him that the modern man was from another planet, with his bows of glass, of plastic, of metal—his arrows of the same diversified materials. And should the two meet in competition, I fear the old archer would suffer. With the new equipment has come a change in shooting techniques—so that today's average archer could in all probability shoot rings around his opposite number of forty years ago. The average good girl archer in high school today, would, in all probability, score more golds than any man who stood on the fields of Crecy, Poitiers or Agincourt. The modern bowman and bow-woman are experts in an old, old field. •

British Army is only one in world today with a unit of archers: they act as Queen's bodyguard.

Photo by Picture Post, London, through PIX, Inc.

A 35-pound bow is sufficient for all target work, but most amateurs buy much heavier bows.

SELECTION OF EQUIPMENT

Over-bowing himself is the biggest mistake the aspiring archer can make: it's not the strength of the bow that counts as much as the way it's used.

Victor De Palma from Free-Lance Photographers Guild

SELECTION OF EQUIPMENT

ONE of the first things anyone has to learn about archery is the proper selection of equipment. If you want to go trout fishing, you don't buy a tuna rig. And if you go on an African safari, you don't depend on a .22 rifle. The selection of the proper tackle in archery is, strangely enough, even more important than either of these, if you want to really enjoy the sport.

Many of us make the grave error of selecting a bow that is far too heavy. Called over-bowing, it is one of the cardinal sins of the game. In the first place, a bow pulling seventy-five pounds (in archery the pull of the bow is determined by the pounds of energy required to bring the bow to full draw) isn't necessary, except under very special circumstances. The average man feels he has to select a heavy bow in order to prove his manhood. And that's a fallacy—from beginning to end. A forty-five pound bow will kill most game just as easily as a seventy-five.

Most of us, buying a first bow, forget that much practice is needed before we can step into the field and bring down our first game. And in those long hours of practice, a difference of five pounds between bows can mean an awful lot. We'll assume that you're new to the game. You're big and strong. You've probably been active in one form of athletics or another. The idea that you should choose a bow with a maximum pull of thirty-five pounds, seems ridiculous. You pick up a bow that pulls sixty pounds and you draw it, easily. A lot of us take that sixty-pound bow—and regret it.

Proper length of an arrow for target archery is measured in this manner: it should reach just the tips of the fingers when its butt end is against neck.

Courtesy Paul Will

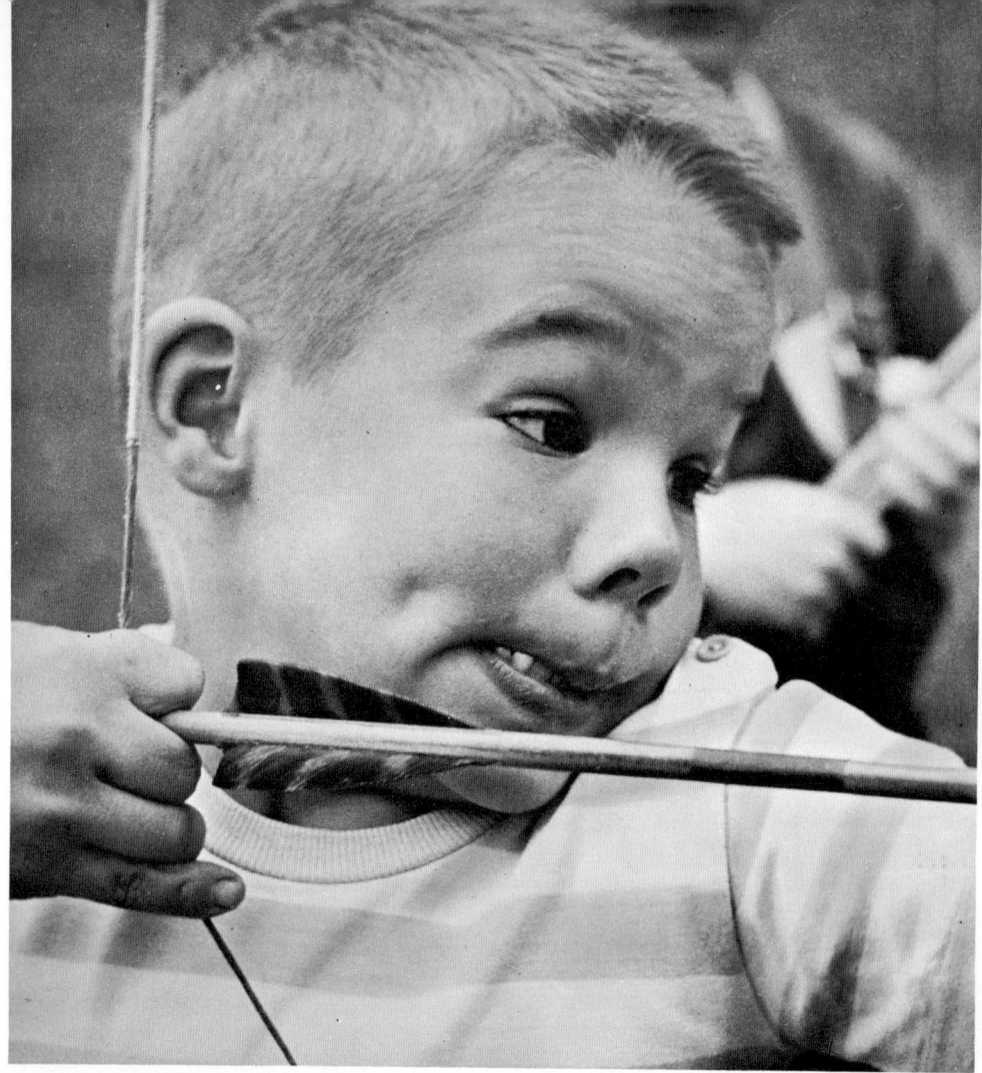

Tharpe from Monkmeyer Press Service

This young lad is obviously an intense archer, but he is breaking all the rules of the game: no one, if he wants to be accurate, clutches an arrow-nock against string; it is held lightly with fingertips.

There are two reasons for that regret. The more important is this—if you are over-bowed, you cannot concentrate on the essentials, which must become automatic before you can hope to become a successful archer. It's much, much easier to select a light bow for beginning and then advance to the heavy level. That first bow must become a part of you, an unconscious extension of your arms. You cannot worry about aching muscles, pinched fingers and the like if you hope to be good. Time will come, soon enough, when you can take the big one out and use it. But for a beginning—be sensible. Remember the best archers in the world aren't out to break any records for maximum pull.

The second reason for keeping the bow light, and it ties in directly with the first, is this: use simple arithmetic to see what five pounds of difference in a bow can mean in the course of an afternoon. Suppose, for example, you go out to practice with a sixty-pound bow. In the course of an afternoon you shoot ninety arrows—which will mean that you have exerted 5,400 pounds of energy (every time you pull a bow you exert its weight). The man next to you, who is using a bow with a thirty-five-pound pull, shot the same number of arrows and only exerted 3,150 pounds of energy. Odds are, he scored just as high, if not higher than you did. And in comparison —you performed the equivalent of shovel-

SELECTION OF EQUIPMENT

ing two and one-half tons of coal, while he shoveled a little over a ton and a half. Most of us aren't in condition to do that much work, particularly without a period of conditioning. So remember, even if you insist on a heavy bow, break yourself in gently—you'll enjoy it more in the long run.

Next to your selection of a bow, the selection of arrows is the most important factor in getting started. In fact, many archers feel that it's better to have good arrows and an inexpensive bow, than vice versa. It follows that a good bow, with the best of design and construction, cannot make a bad arrow fly true, whereas an inexpensive bow can and will drive good arrows into the spot you aim for.

Arrows are selected on the basis of two factors. (Flight arrows, which we'll discuss later, are in a highly specialized category and aren't considered here.) Those considerations are length and spine. An arrow should be the right length to suit the archer. Just as a good fly rod is part and parcel of its owner, so archery equipment is adjusted to its user. And just as an aside, because of this and for pure courtesy, don't use someone else's equipment, unless the emergency is dire.

To judge the proper length of your arrow, you need only the simplest equipment—the common yardstick. Lacking that, a long straight stick will do just as well. Place the end against your armpit (right arm if you are right handed and left arm if you are a southpaw). Push your arm up and out until it's straight and level with your shoulder. Mark the position of the second joint of your index finger on your yardstick or straightedge and you have the correct arrow length for your arm. This length allows you to draw to a point under your chin, which is the usual target practice. In field shooting, and in hunting, many archers prefer to have the anchor point (see section on actual shooting for details on selection of anchor point) farther back, along the side of the jaw. If you wish to follow that practice, allow two inches more than the measure shows. The greatest danger in archery is over-drawing the bow, i.e. pulling the arrow too far back. Once you've established your anchor point your arrow length is also set and you don't run so much risk. If you want to make arrows for the younger members of the family, get them a couple of inches longer than the child's arm actually calls for. A child doesn't always draw to the same spot and the extra length will lessen the chances of over-drawing.

Although it may be a trifle out of place,

Photo by Anthony Lane
Courtesy Paul Bunyan Bait Co

Courtesy Paul Bunyan Bait Co.

Hunting bows, by state law, must be at least of 45-pound pull. Advice: don't start off with this!

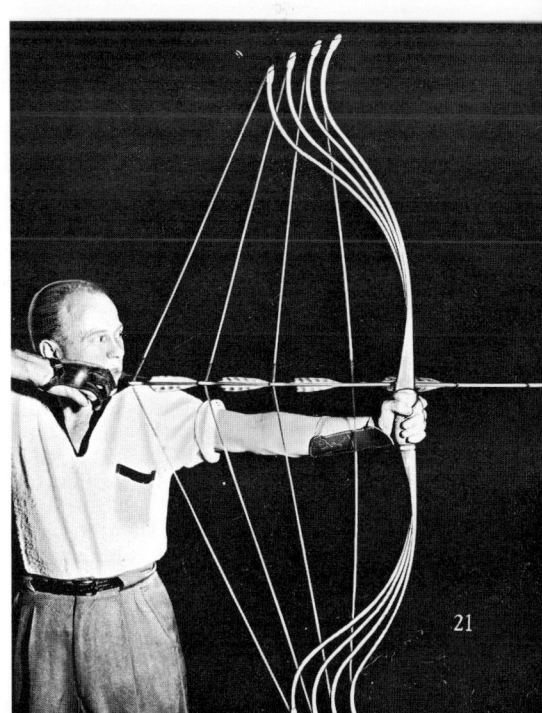

Stroboscopic photo showing action of arrow as it is released, this proves accuracy of right technique.

Hal H. Harrison from Monkmeyer Press Service

Field archers using reflex-type bows, this group is working out in the Pennsylvania Archery Preserve, which that state has set aside for development of the sport. Bow-hunting is exceptionally popular today.

this is as good a spot as any to explain the dangers involved in over-drawing. In the first place, the string may snap allowing the bow to fly free and possibly break. A broken bow can be an ugly thing but by far the greater danger lies in a splintered arrow resulting from an over-draw. As the arrow comes back past the normal point the head may catch against the belly of the bow (which is the side toward the archer) and when the string is released all the pent-up force shatters the arrow so that dangerous splinters fly in all directions. Fortunately, care in the selection of equipment and the observance of fundamental safety practices when shooting reduce the chances of accidents to almost the vanishing point. But always remember,

don't over-draw that bow, no matter how good an archer you are.

The second factor in choosing arrows is something called spine. The spine of an arrow covers two things—the arrow's stiffness and its flexibility. It may not make sense to say an arrow must be stiff and flexible at one and the same time, but the fact remains. An arrow that is too stiff (and this generally means too thick as well) will hit against the side of the bow as you release the string. Because of this stiffness, the arrow will not resume its course in the direction in which you have aimed it and will fly wide to the left (if you are shooting right handed).

Conversely, if the arrow is too limber, when it is released it buckles, assuming a

SELECTION OF EQUIPMENT

Free-Lance Photographers Guild

Howard Hill, world-famous champion archer, demonstrates his versatility with longbow. Amateurs shouldn't try it!

bend as it starts its flight. And it's just as hard to send an arrow true to the mark if it's too limber, as it is when it's too stiff. You may have the best arrows in the world, but unless they match your bow, your chances of being consistent are nil.

When you're after consistency—and who isn't—you should remember that the arrows you shoot must match. If one arrow is too stiff, you may compensate when you shoot the second, but unless that second arrow is just as stiff, you will have overcompensated. The same thing, of course, holds true for arrows that are too limber.

In general, you can do a decent job of selecting arrows for spine by their diameter. If you buy commercial arrows, the maker usually indicates the proper bow weight for the shafts. Look for his markings; or ask the sales clerk about weights.

Essentially these are the main points to be remembered when you start acquiring archery tackle. There are other things to take into consideration, as you progress, but basically you need only remember:

- **Don't over-bow yourself.**
- **Get, or make, the best arrows you possibly can.**
- **Be sure that the arrows are your length. The clerk in the store isn't going to shoot them—you are.**
- **Be sure that the arrows you use are right for your bow.**

It cannot be emphasized too strongly that you keep these rules in mind. •

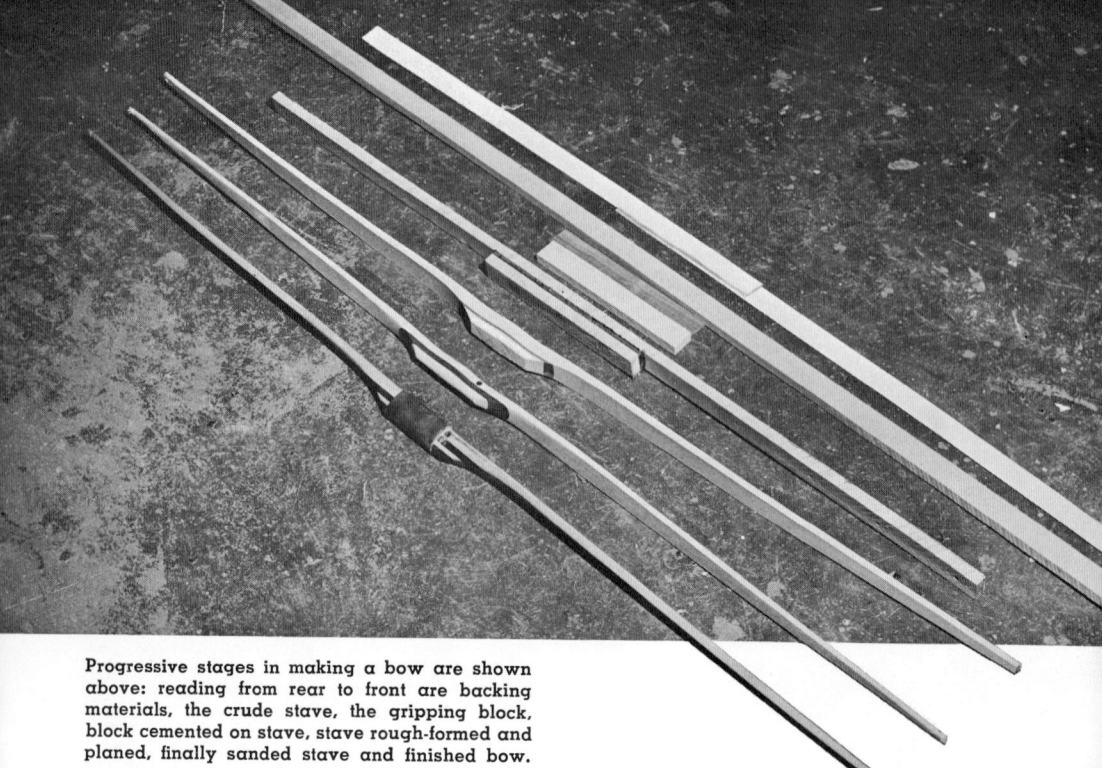

Progressive stages in making a bow are shown above: reading from rear to front are backing materials, the crude stave, the gripping block, block cemented on stave, stave rough-formed and planed, finally sanded stave and finished bow.

Bow Making

It's easier than you may think to make a well-balanced bow, although careful workmanship is necessary. Tips on double-checking as you work are given here.

YOU'RE ready now, we hope, to start making your first bow. But before you go too far, it might be wise to inquire into the subject of bows in general. Bow-making is simple—it requires few tools and little ingenuity. As a matter of fact, it's possible to make a bow with a hatchet and some broken glass, but we'll work under the assumption that such a procedure is unnecessarily crude.

First let's look at the bow and get in mind the terms used to describe it—no matter what its type. These names are traditional and no bow, worth the name, lacks them.

As you hold a bow in your hand, it is perpendicular to the ground. See Diagram A. Your hand is around the grip or handle (A) the portion extending upward from your arm is called the upper limb (B). The portion that goes toward the floor (C) is the lower limb. In most bows the upper limb is slightly longer than the lower. At either end of the bow, at the top and bottom are two recesses (D and E) called the upper and lower nocks. These hold the bowstring in place when the bow is strung. The portion of the bow toward the shooter is called the belly (F) and the outer side of the bow is called the back (G).

With the general terms for a bow in mind, let us now examine the types of bows, with the idea that one of them will serve as our first attempt at the art of bow-making. The most famous bow in the

Photos in this chapter by Hal Kelly

BOW MAKING

Basic diagram showing parts of bow: use this to relate with rough stave so you can make markings.

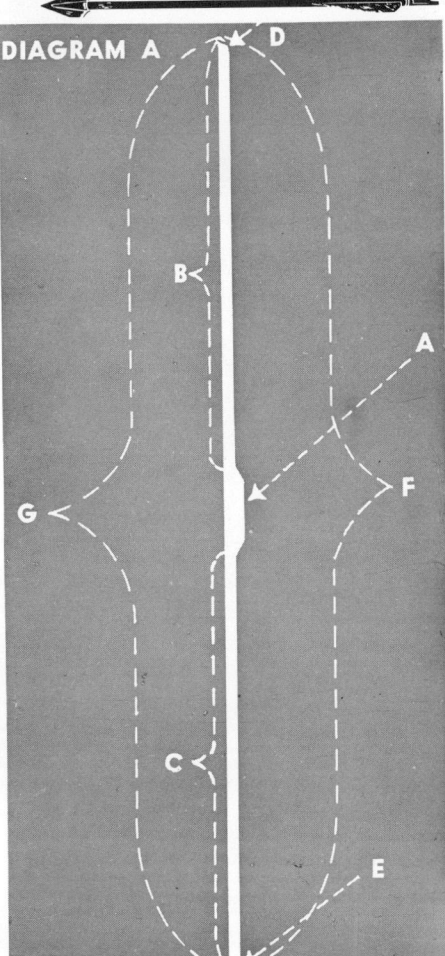

First step: stave in vise, handle blocks cemented in place with strong glue and clamped tightly till dry.

English language is, of course, the long bow. Centuries old, the long bow seems to have been developed originally in Wales. Hundreds of thousands of long bows have been made and will be made, although the modern archer finds fault with their performance. A long bow shoots well—smoothly and without harshness—or as the archer says "sweetly." Unfortunately, the long bow lacks what is called cast—an arrow shot from a bow lacking cast does not have the same velocity as one from a bow with this highly desirable quality. For short ranges, up to approximately 60 yards, the long bow is a thing of beauty, but beyond that point its loss of cast makes it a less desirable weapon.

The American Indian used a form of bow corresponding to our modern flat bow. Because of its simple construction and extreme cast, the flat bow became very

ARROW LENGTH TO BOW LENGTH (FLAT BOW)	
ARROW	BOW
25"	5' 0"
26"	5' 4"
27"	5' 7"
28"	5' 9"

Stave is marked off with pencil and plumb line before planing. Here, half-finished stave is used as guide.

popular. It is the only bow that follows a mathematical formula in its construction. In cross section the flat bow is a rectangle, four times as broad as it is thick, the proportions holding true at any point along either limb. The greatest drawback in the flat bow is the fact that it is so short, usually, that when it is full drawn the string forms a very acute angle around the fingers, pinching them and making a clean loose next to impossible.

The ideal bow is light in the hand, smooth in action, with good cast, no finger-pinch and capable of performing over long periods of time. The design of the long bow, in cross section looks sort of like an inverted top. The back and the belly are relatively small, in comparison to the total area. When engineers approached the subject of bow-design they found that the area between the belly and the back was "dead wood." The bow in shooting is subject to two distinct and equal forces. The back must sustain a tremendous amount of stretch, while simultaneously the belly undergoes an equal amount of compression. The center area remains inert, serving only to hold the back and belly in position. Breakage in a bow usually occurs in the back, in the form of splintering and in the belly in the form of fretting. Frets or crystals are minute lateral fractures along the belly of the bow, caused by the strain of compression, which fractures the fibers. See Diagram B, **Showing: Cross section of long bow, cross section of stacked yew bow, cross section of flat bow and cross section of rectangular bow—with stress indicated on cross sections.**

In redesigning bows it was necessary to eliminate bulk in the center—the deadwood area—for lightness and to increase the effective area of the belly. The back was already adequate, the belly needed correction to prevent fretting and to achieve a bow with a balanced ratio of compression and stretch. The resultant cross section, that of a trapezoidal bow, is,

BOW MAKING

DIAGRAM B—C

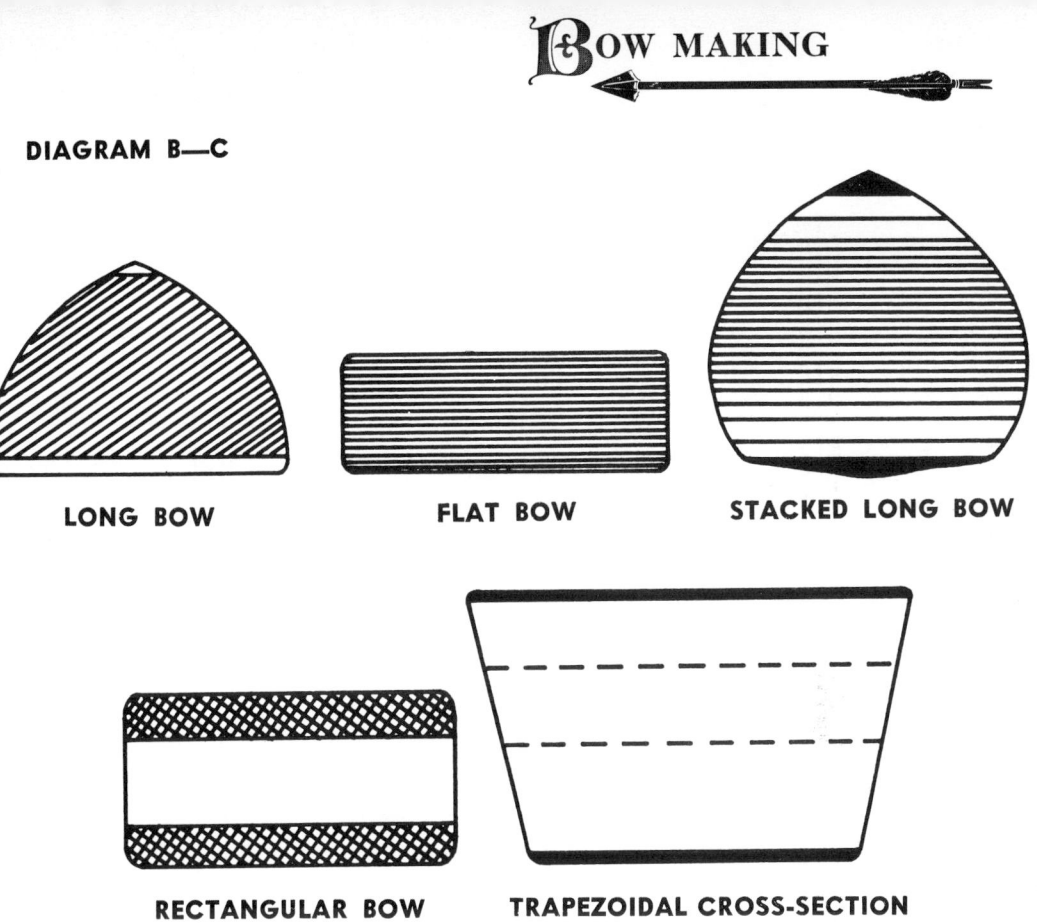

LONG BOW FLAT BOW STACKED LONG BOW

RECTANGULAR BOW TRAPEZOIDAL CROSS-SECTION

from a standpoint of design, the finest in the world for performance. See Diagram C.

Before we go into the actual directions for making either a flat bow or a long bow, we'll have to consider what wood should be used. There are many woods that have been used in bow making, and there are numerous woods, particularly from the tropics, which may some day prove to be good. But essentially there are only two great bow woods—yew and osage orange. Frankly, neither of them is suitable for experimentation, when you're making your first bow.

Yew is the most famous of all the bow woods. A relative of the evergreens, it occurs in the United States only in our Pacific Northwest. The trees grow very slowly, are difficult to find and often are faulty when cut. The wood has two parts, the thin, white sapwood and the dark heartwood. Seemingly, when Nature created the yew, she had the archer in mind, for the heartwood is ideally suited to withstand the strains of compression, while the sapwood is equally superb for stretch. But because of these very facts, each stave or billet must be treated with respect and caution so that the rind or sapwood forms the thin back and the dark heartwood makes the belly. In addition, the wood is subject to a twisted grain, which must be followed when making a bow. All in all, the yew is a wonderful bow wood, but extremely difficult to work and cannot be recommended for your first attempt.

Osage orange is the second of the great bow woods. Strictly indigenous to the United States (yew occurs in Europe), it is often called hedge apple or "bow dark," from the French *bois d'arc*. It is the most difficult of all woods to work, because of the fact that it has wide rings, indicating annual growth, and the rings are composed of two distinct woods—one hard and the other pithy. It cannot be glued without special treatment and the grain prevents its being planed or shaved. On the credit

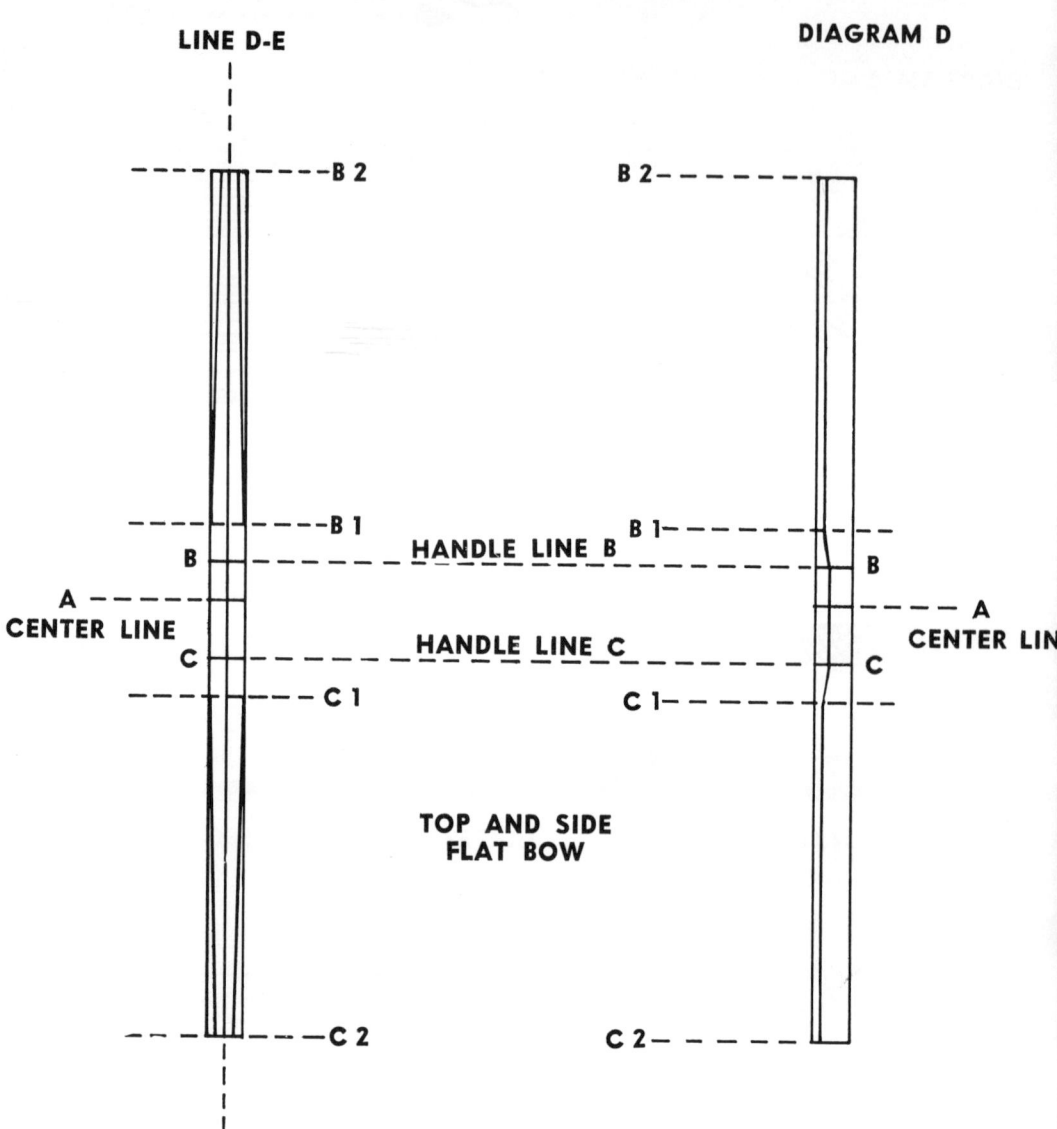

DIAGRAM D

TOP AND SIDE FLAT BOW

side of the ledger, osage is sturdy, has terrific cast and is pre-eminent in the making of hunting or field bows. Unlike yew, temperature changes do not affect it adversely but again, it is not a wood for experimentation. Save it, along with the good yew stave, for a later bow.

Having momentarily put aside the most famous woods, let's look at the ones which are readily usable. Foremost of these is lemonwood, so called because of its color. It is not related to the fruit. Another name for this wood is dagame. Most lemonwood comes from Cuba, although it occurs throughout most of the Caribbean. The grain in lemonwood is so fine that it is difficult to see with the naked eye and bowyers are able to work it without paying attention to the grain at all—a far cry from working with osage or yew. The wood planes well, takes a good finish and has the added advantage of being one of the least expensive of the bow woods. The vast majority of bows made by beginners are cut from lemonwood and most factory-produced bows are made from it. Its only drawbacks are: a tendency to dry out and go brittle over a winter, a tendency to fol-

BOW MAKING

In making laminated bow (not recommended for amateurs) each lamination is cemented, clamped to dry.

low the string (when the bow is unstrung it does not return fully to its original shape) and an inability to perform properly in cold weather. Interestingly, lemonwood contains no natural resins and so can never be used for making a reflex bow.

Another, even more common, wood can be used for bows—and that is hickory. Many American Indians used this wood for their bows and it makes a tough and inexpensive hunting bow, capable of standing all kinds of knocking around, which would ruin a piece of yew. It, too, has a tendency to follow the string and is slow, having a poor cast. But it is not to be discounted as a bow wood, particularly for a first try, since it is very inexpensive.

As we've already pointed out, your arrows should fit you and your bow should fit your arrows. It does you no good to shoot a twenty-seven-inch arrow with a bow that measures six-foot-three. In making a modified flat-bow, the chart on page 25 will serve as a guide in selecting the proper length of bow stave.

It's well to bear in mind that the flat bows are relatively short, so that a completed bow five feet long may well be the equivalent, in pull, to a long bow of six feet or over. The width of the limb in the flat-bow is the governing factor in the over-all length, within limits.

Select a stave of the proper length, from the chart. The wood should be 1½ inches wide and approximately ¾ of an inch thick. Your stave should be as straight as possible, but if there are slight bends they can be corrected by steaming. Don't try to straighten the entire length of a stave at one time. Apply steam to one small area

A bandsaw is very helpful in cutting out shape of bow if it is complicated recurve or fancy. Below is diagram of simple tiller, use of which is described in story. Facing page shows shaper being used to shape handle.

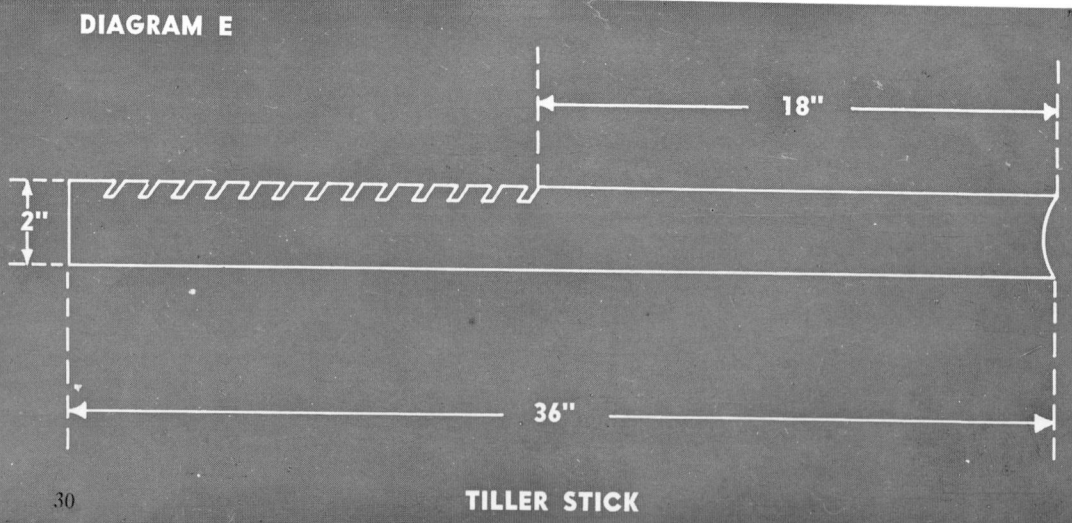

DIAGRAM E

2"

18"

36"

TILLER STICK

BOW MAKING

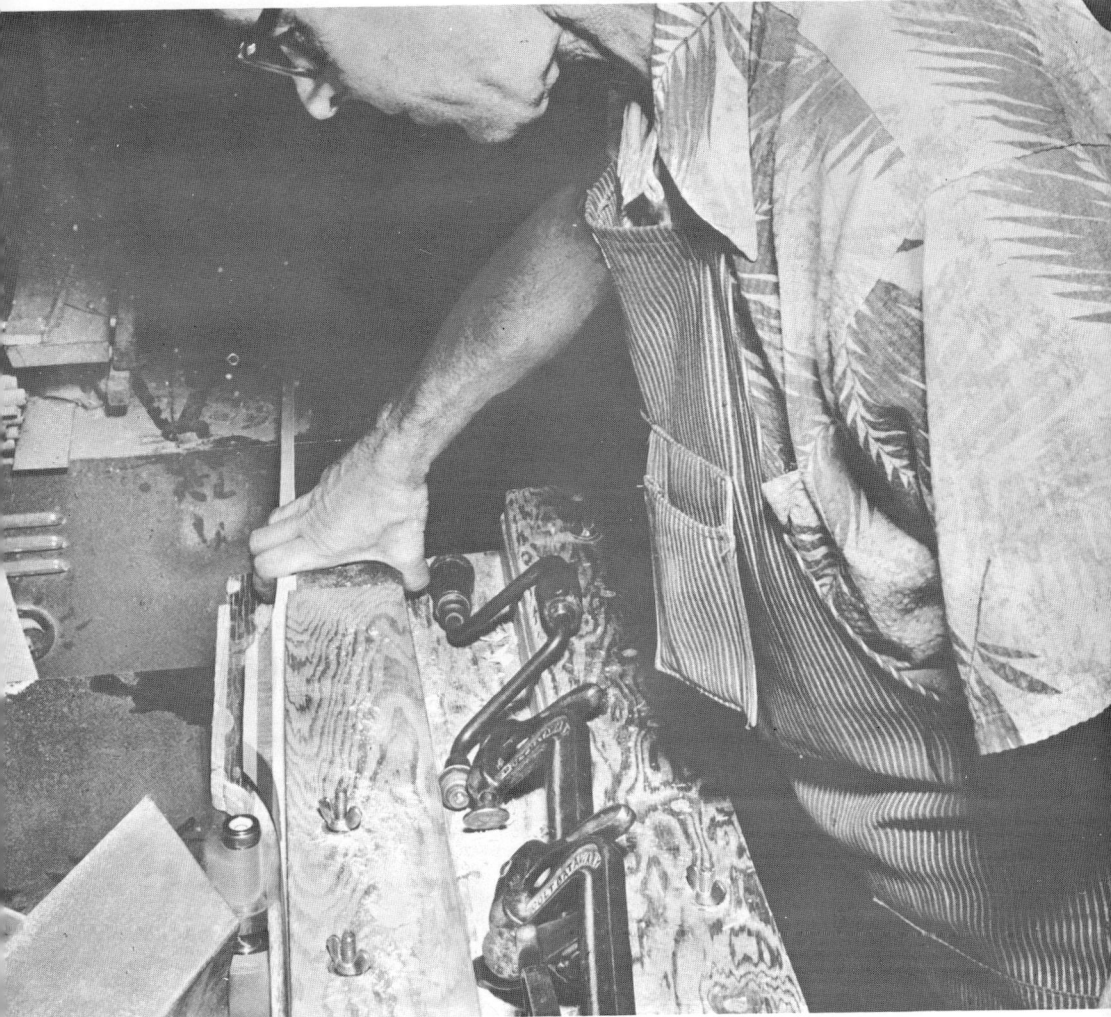

If you have a shaper in your workshop it will speed up handle-shaping; if not, a small plane will do.

and straighten that before you move on to the next crooked spot. When you are satisfied the stave is as straight as you can get it, lay it on a flat surface and plane one side smooth. Don't work too deeply, but simply remove saw marks or any other surface imperfections.

This will form the back of your bow and you are now ready to lay out the pattern on your smooth surface.

Diagram D on page 28 shows flat stave with the pattern drawn on—top and side views.

First, mark the exact center (A) of the stave. Continue this line around the wood. Next mark a point (B) an inch and a quarter above the center line and a second point (C) two and three quarters inches below the center point. Continue these two lines all the way around the bow. They mark the position of the handle. Next draw a line exactly down the center of the back of the bow (D-E).

Using line D-E and line A, proceed to mark out the pattern on the back. The hand grip, from line B to line C should be ¾ of an inch wide. At six inches up and down along line D-E allow the back to swell out to a width of 1 and $\frac{7}{32}$ inches on the upper limb and 1 and ⅛ inches on the lower. Six inches farther out, or a total of twelve inches up and down from line A, both

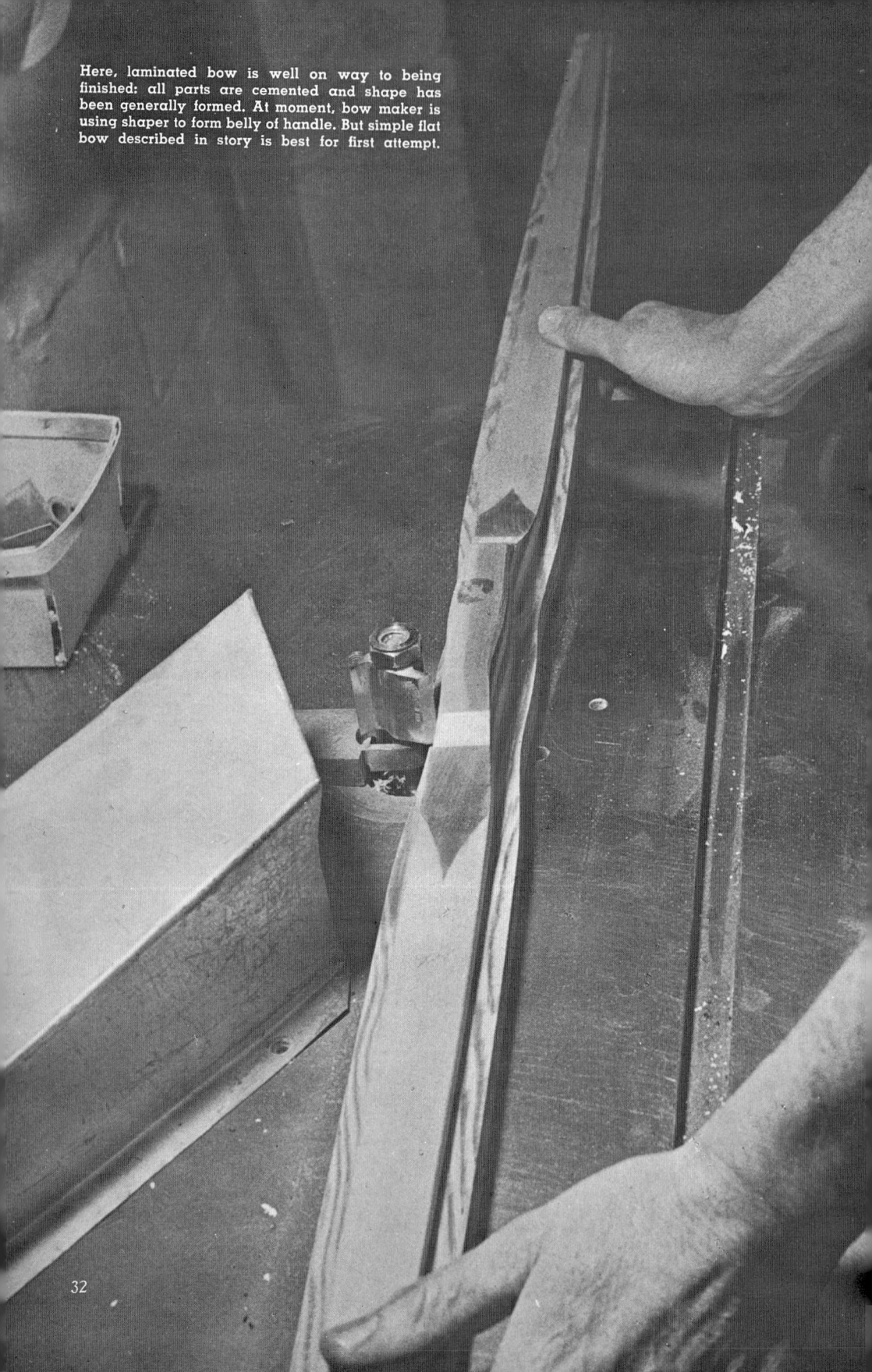

Here, laminated bow is well on way to being finished: all parts are cemented and shape has been generally formed. At moment, bow maker is using shaper to form belly of handle. But simple flat bow described in story is best for first attempt.

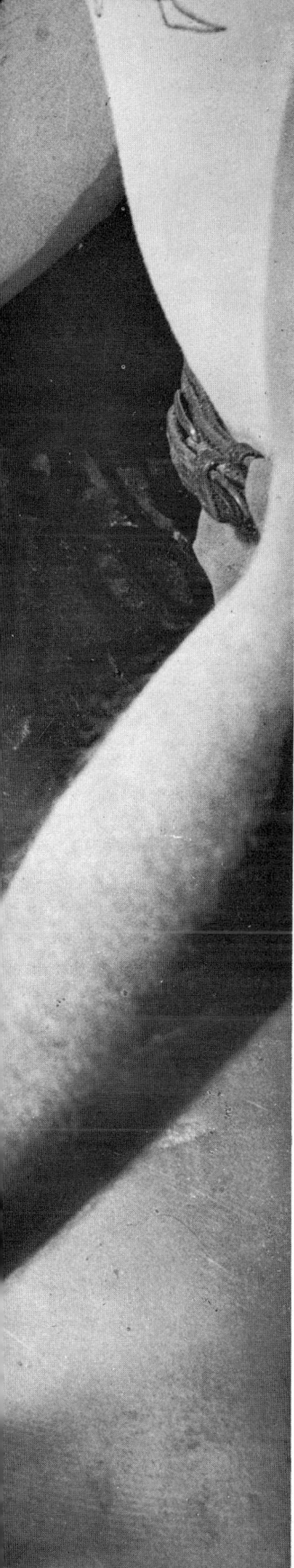

limbs should have a breadth of 1 and $\tfrac{7}{32}$ inches. From that point they taper in until at the end of the stave they measure ⅜ of an inch. This taper should be brought in gradually, so that both limbs are in perfect symmetry.

If you are using lemonwood or hickory you can follow these outlines with a band-saw, a plane or a draw-shave. A handy man with a hatchet can follow the pattern, too, but don't make the mistake of cutting too deep, no matter what your tool. There should be no knots in either of these woods, but if you do run across any, leave a little extra wood around them to compensate for any weakness in the area.

The next step is to cut the other taper and here even more care must be exercised. For it is in taking down the belly that you either make or break a bow. It is far, far easier to take wood off, than it is to put it back. If you should take off too much in an area, you can back the bow with rawhide, or one of the new plastic backings or you can take a little off either end, shortening the bow and giving it more strength. But as you shorten a bow, you greatly increase your chances of breaking it.

Again referring to our lines A and D-E, the taper of the belly should run as follows: on the upper limb, at a distance six inches above the center, the bow should be ⅝ in. through and at six inches below center, $\tfrac{13}{16}$ in. At one foot up and down the through dimension is equal, $\tfrac{9}{16}$ in. As on the other side, the taper begins here and is brought gradually to the end, where the bow should measure ⅜ in. thick.

Before you begin to remove the excess from the belly it's a good plan to put in your nocks. Set them in about ¾ of an inch from either end, using a rattail file for the purpose. You will need to string and draw the bow during the process of cutting out the belly, and the nocks are necessary. Get a good strong bow-string for this purpose—one stressed to take a lot more weight than your finished bow will pull.

The next stage in cutting the belly is called tillering and you may be certain, is the most delicate part of bow making. A tiller is a simple mechanical device to let you see how the arc of the bow is taking shape. The simplest tiller of all is a piece of wood roughly thirty-six inches long, two inches wide and a half inch thick. In one end of this stick cut a groove to hold the bow handle and down one side cut a set of notches, spaced at inch intervals, starting at eighteen inches and continuing out to the end opposite the groove. See

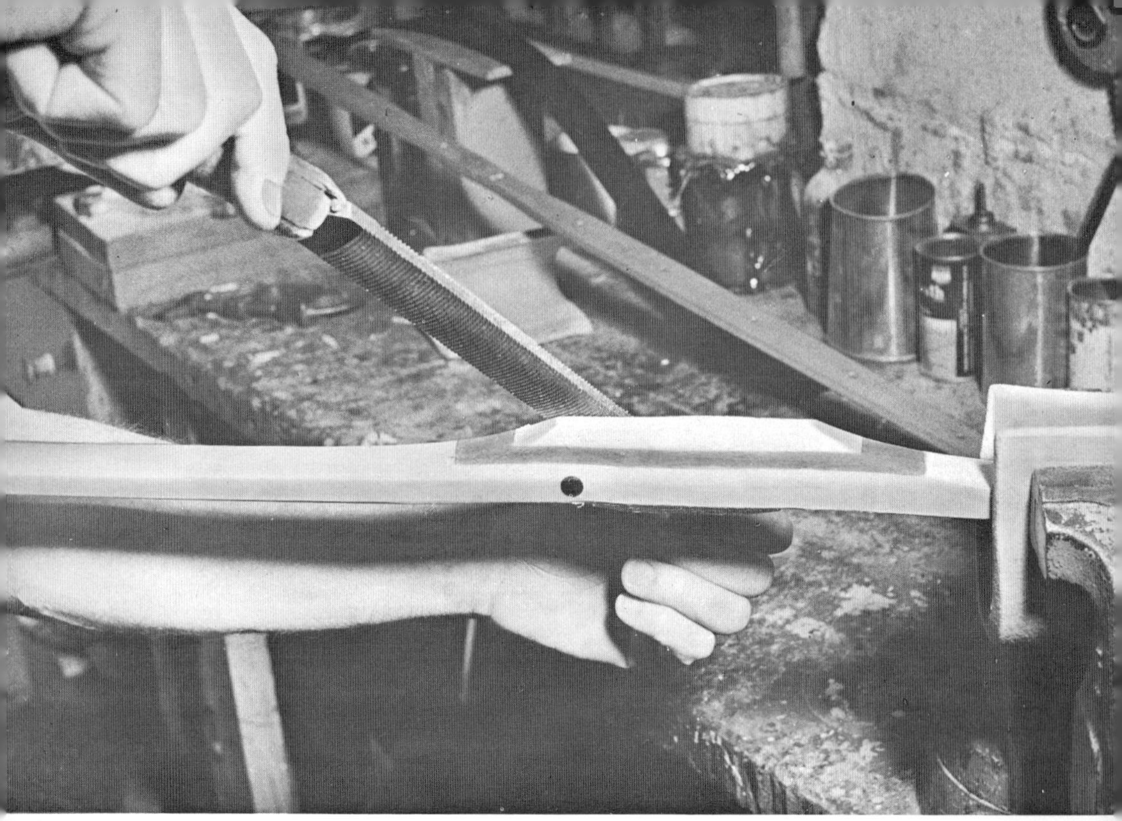

Filing is an intermediary step after grip has been rough-shaped. Hold bow firmly in vise and work gently. Sanding comes next, as shown below. Again, work gently. If too much wood is filed or sanded away in one spot, entire bow will have to be thinned down to keep balance. Diagram, right, shows basic bow-parts.

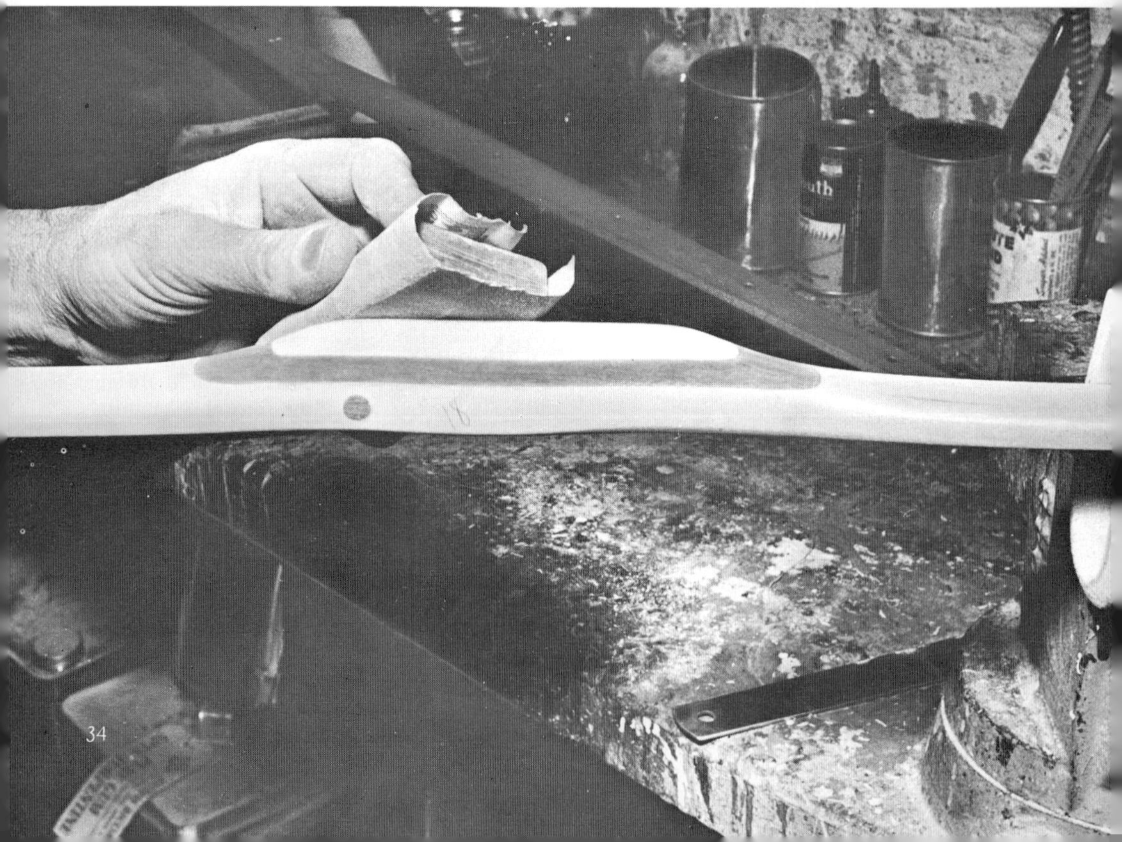

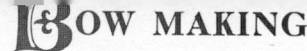# BOW MAKING

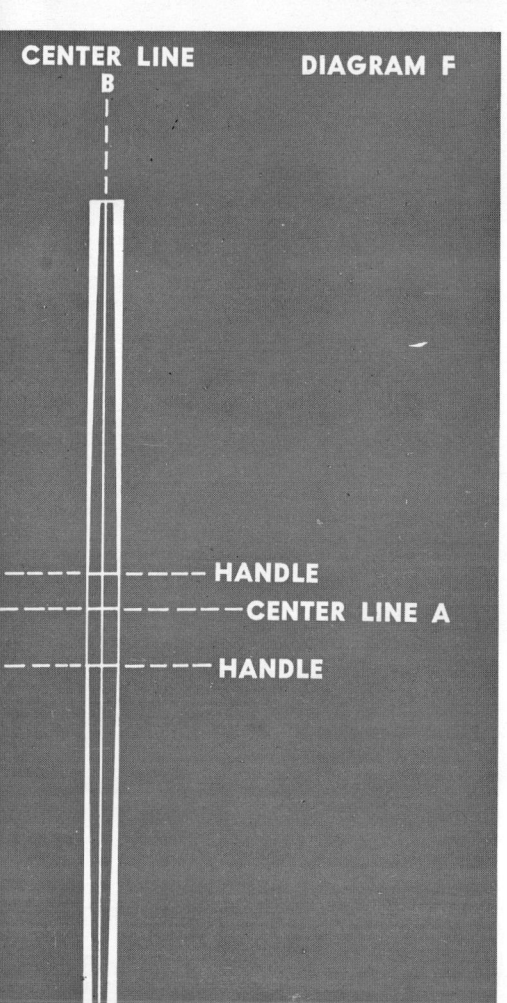

in the jaws of a padded vise before it can be strung. Be very careful at this point for it is easy to break the bow.

With the string in place insert the tiller between the handle and the string, putting the string in the first of the notches. If you have good eyes and can judge properly, you can now see whether or not the two limbs are taking the same amount of bend. Remember that the upper limb is slightly longer than the lower, and consequently, when braced the string is a fraction of an inch farther from that limb than the lower. If you don't trust your judgment, draw a chalk line grid on the floor and lay the tillered bow down on it, so that you can see the exact intersection of the two limbs in relation to the grid.

Take a soft pencil and mark those spots along either limb where the bend is noticeably stiffer. Remove the tiller, unstring the bow and go back to work with your drawshave. Go gently and when you think you don't have quite enough wood removed, tiller it again. As you take the excess wood off the belly, remember to keep the cross section indicated in the first pattern. As you take out the stiff places, be careful to leave your surfaces flat and free from deep gauges or cuts. Once a cut is in a bow limb the only way to adjust is to reduce all the remaining area of the bow, and you may lose too much weight.

Repeat the tillering and scraping until you have about a twenty-six-inch draw set up on the tiller stick and your limbs bend uniformly throughout their length. Your next step will be to determine the draw or pull of the bow. It is not essential to wait until this point to do so, but many bowyers prefer to follow this method.

Set your bow in position firmly and attach a spring scale to the string. Pull back slowly until you reach your twenty-six-inch draw. The reading on the scale will tell you your draw. Be careful as you are doing this, since it's all too easy to overdraw. If the weight is acceptable, you're ready to finish the bow. If it is too heavy, you'll have to work the limbs down even more, taking care to maintain the proper proportions throughout their lengths. *Do not touch the handle.* Remember that the bow does not bend at the handle. It does not come full circle when you draw, but rather the two limbs, above and below the handle, curve in two arcs. To touch the handle is to weaken it, and consequently the whole bow.

The handle is finished by gluing a piece

page 30 for diagram of tiller stick from side. It's easy to make a tiller.

Preliminary removal of excess belly wood should be done now and when you have come fairly close to the pattern lines, stop and string your bow. Use a string with a single loop (which should be placed in the upper nock). The bottom of the string, which will be in the lower nock, is fastened with a timber hitch, and adjusted according to the length of the bow and the amount of brace that you want to give it as you are tillering. Since at this point the bow is much heavier than it will be later, it may be difficult to string it, without help of one sort or another. If someone is around to help, the problem is easy, but it is often necessary, if you're alone, to put the bow

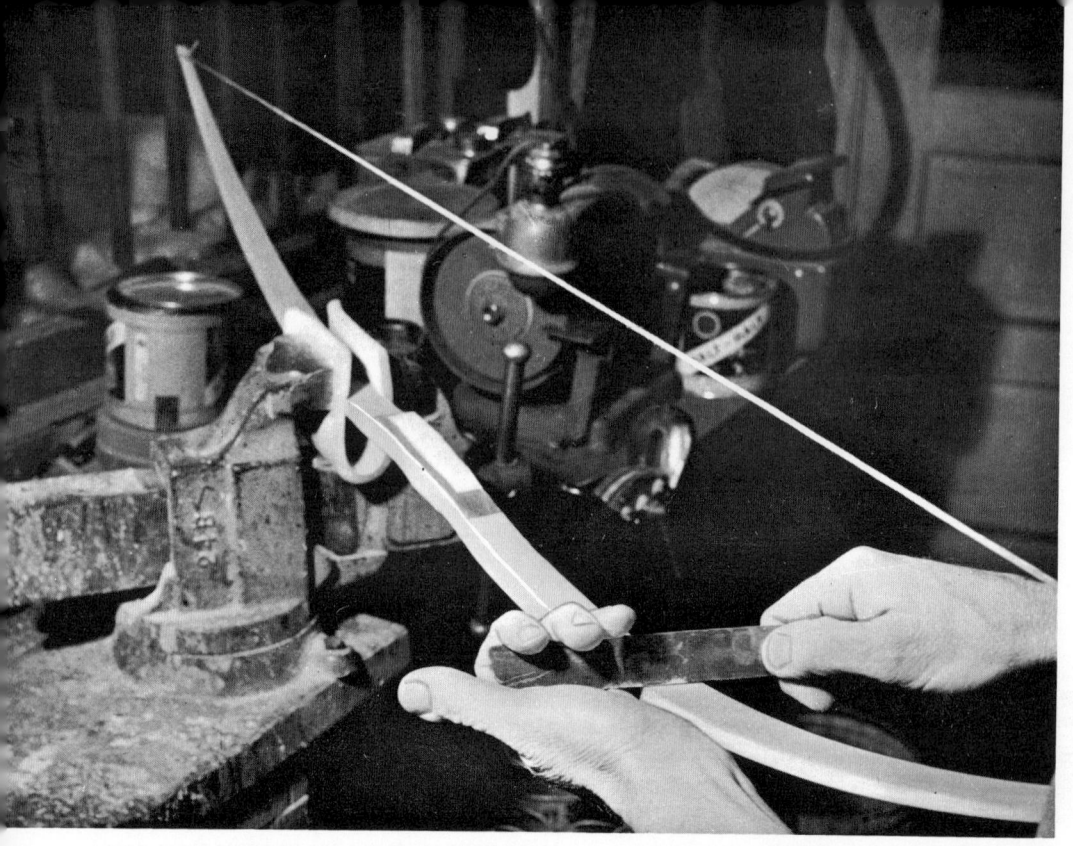

When nearly finished, bow should be strung and tested from time to time. Clamp between folded leather for protection in vise and use scraper carefully on the belly until a proper balance has been reached.

of wood to *the back*, not the belly, at the grip. The wood should be the same size as the actual handle and thick enough to allow you to cut a full hand grip. The grip may be of simple form or ornate— according to your wishes.

Sand the whole bow smooth and apply a good coat of varnish. Allow it to dry for at least forty-eight hours, then smooth again with fine-grade steel wool. Apply a second coating of varnish and allow this to dry perfectly before smoothing and polishing.

A second type of finish, and one that many people prefer is linseed oil. The boiled oil is preferable. Smear the bow with oil and rub it in with your finger tips. If the wood doesn't soak up all the oil, wipe the remainder off with a soft cloth, then hang the bow up for a day or two. Repeat several times, or until the wood refuses to absorb any more oil. When the surface of the wood is free from any oil, rub it thoroughly with a soft cloth. The resulting finish is a thing of beauty and will keep any moisture out of the bow. It has the advantage of being in the wood and not on it. At any future time you can repeat the procedure, insuring that the bow is constantly moisture proof.

Finishing the handle is somewhat complicated. You and you alone can decide how much time and effort you'll want to spend in this step. Incidentally, the finish of a handle is the same for both the long bow and the flat bow, so the description will not be repeated. The simplest method of finishing your handle is to smear the area with glue and wrap it from end to end with stout line, or light cord. When you've finished wrapping the handle, secure the ends, wipe off any excess glue and allow to dry. It isn't the prettiest finish possible, but it is serviceable and will serve to give you a more than adequate grip.

If you really want to do a professional job, you should add an arrow rest and an arrow plate to the handle assembly. The first is simply a ledge set on the side of the handle, on which the arrow rests during draw. It serves a double purpose, keeping the arrow at the same point on the bow whenever you shoot and preventing the shooter from getting feather cuts as the shaft flies over the top of the hand. The arrow plate is simply a cushion, either set flush with the side of the bow just above the arrow rest or raised slightly above the surface of the wood. Again, it serves to

BOW MAKING

DIAGRAM G

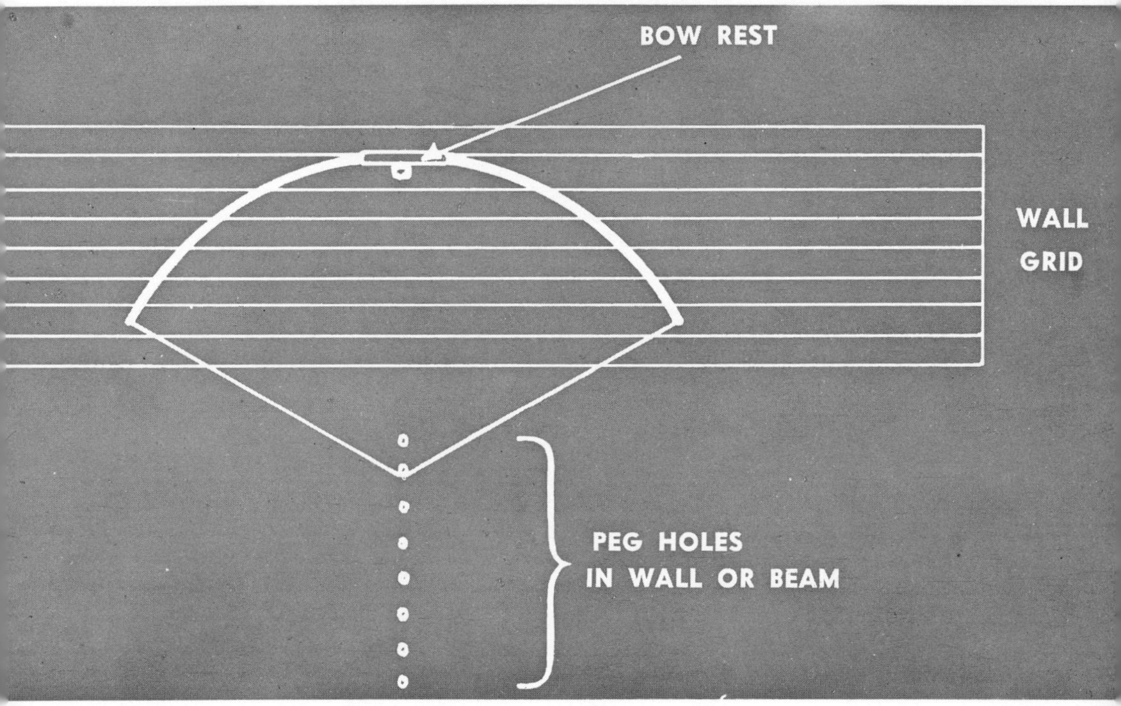

BOW REST

WALL GRID

PEG HOLES IN WALL OR BEAM

guide you in seeing that your arrow is always in the same place and also deadens the sound of the arrow as it slaps over the bow. The latter is important in hunting, for that tiny sound can frighten more game than you'd dream possible. For range work, the arrow plate is either of contrasting hard wood or fiber; on hunting and field bows it is almost universally made of soft leather.

Cut your arrow rest from wood and glue in place along the side of the grip. It should flare out above your hand, giving you a shelf of approximately 3/8 of an inch width. After the glue is set, sand the entire grip until it is perfectly smooth. I personally like to finish a bow with leather, having a moderately rough surface. You can use one piece, as long as your handle, or a spiral binding with leather may suit you. With the single piece, cut it so that the two edges will meet exactly in the middle of the back. Shave the edges so that when they meet there is no abrupt edge. Let your leather soak in water until it is completely pliable. When it is thoroughly wet take it out of the water and wring it dry. Smear the handle with a good glue, preferably a casein type, using enough for a good hold, but not an excess. Place the leather in position, smooth and wrap the whole area with surgical gauze, keeping a steady pressure at all times. Since the glue is slow to dry, you may unroll the bandage after a half hour and check the position of the leather. If it needs change, adjust it, rewrap and let dry overnight.

If you're putting a leather arrow rest on the bow, it can be done at the same time, using the same glue and wrapping. The leather should be cut in the form of an oval, so that one side goes up on the bow itself and the bottom rests on the arrow shelf. Check this carefully when you unwind the wrappings as the plate may have a tendency to bunch. Use a very fine grade of leather, so it will lie as flat as possible against the bow.

Making the long bow is simpler than making the flat bow. Your stave should be longer, roughly six feet long and 1⅛ inches square. Examine it carefully for any bending. Most lemonwood is straight, but in case there is a bend in the stave use the concave side for the back of the bow. Plane the stave smooth on all sides and mark off the handle. Again, use a center line, a line 1¼ inches above the center and an-

Final step in making of bow is applying leather handle-grip, which should be cut in oval shape so it can fit easily around arrow rest on bow, cover belly.

other 2¾ inches below it. Carry the three lines completely around the stave. Next mark the back, from end to end, exactly in the middle, being sure that the center line bisects the center line of the grip.

At the top of the limbs draw straight lines across the back and mark out the center section to the width of ¾ of an inch. Next, connect, by lines, the ends of the hand grip sections to the ends of the ¾ inch lines on the corresponding limb.

Diagram F on page 35 shows the layout of the back of a long bow.

Take off the wood that lies outside of these long lines. A plane is preferable since lemonwood does not cut too well with a saw. Keep the cuts even so you have no dips or bends. Then turn the stave on its side and mark off a thickness of ½ inch, at either end, measuring from the *back*. Draw lines from the ends of the hand grips to this set of end lines and again remove the surplus wood. When you finish the stave will be tapered from side to side and from back to belly. Only the hand grip should remain unchanged. Your bow is now taking shape.

The next stages are where your skill with wood will come in handy. The cross section of the long bow (see Diagram B-C, page 27) shows the back forming the flat side. In no case do you alter the flat side, except in the final stages when you take off the sharp edges. But the stave, which you have now tapered must conform to this shape from the hand grip to the ends. Take the wood off gradually and evenly, tillering as you go.

String the bow, as with the flat bow, and check for the following points: the lower limb should be a shade stronger than the upper, because of the difference in length;

BOW MAKING

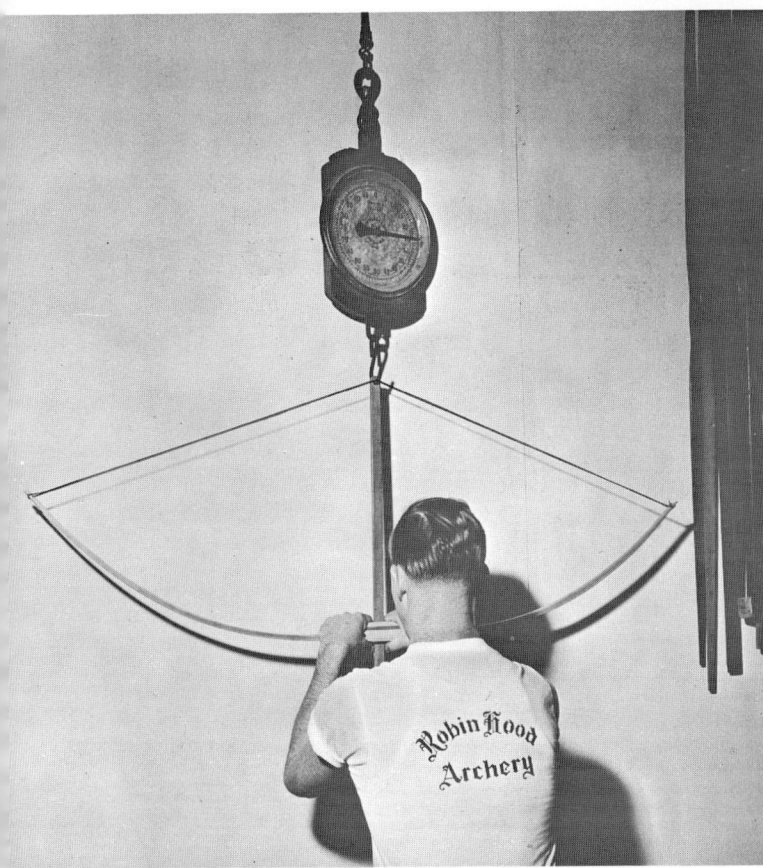

Last test of completed bow is weight or pull test. An ordinary scale may be used as shown, but care must be taken not to overdraw beyond arrow length of bow.

there should be no bend in the grip section (the bend should not start for at least two inches on either side of the four-inch gripping block); the limbs should bend evenly, without bulging or bumping of any sort. Further, when you draw the bow, even fractionally, there should be no hint of twisting in your hand. If the bow does show a tendency to twist, it is probably due to your not having marked the lines straight.

A further check on the way the bow is coming into shape can be gotten by having someone else draw the bow for you so that you can stand off and look at it. Check to see that the bow string bisects the whole length of the stave perfectly, that the whole bow is straight when you look straight at it from the back and that the bend of the bow is a clean arc, with a flat center at the hand grip.

As with the flat bow, tiller and check.

Scrape and tiller, until your bow has come round to the perfect shape. There is no substitute at this stage for careful, painstaking work. When you have the bow conforming perfectly and at the proper weight, finish, either with oil or varnish, fix your handle and your bow is done.

If you have the room, it may be well to build a more permanent tiller, against the wall. The tiller stick described previously is adequate, but if you plan to make more than one bow, a tiller on the wall is a great help. Fix your rest for the bow handle and then set pegs or nails in the wall at the proper distances below. When you come to check the draw of the bow, run a cord from the bow string through an eye, set either on the wall or the floor to the hook of your spring scales. Another nice thing about the wall tiller (see Diagram G, page 37) is the fact that you can keep a permanent grid drawn behind it, for ready reference. •

All the equipment you'll need for string making is shown here: a spool of linen thread, beeswax, a sharp knife and a bobbin of serving thread. Best string material is Barbour's No. 12, fortisan or dacron.

how TO MAKE BOWSTRINGS

It takes patience but no special skill to make fine bowstrings: follow carefully the step-by-step photos on these pages and you'll have no trouble.

THE next part of your equipment we'll consider is the bowstring. The string takes most of the hard knocks in any form of archery and it's the part that will wear out fastest. Commercially made bowstrings are excellent, as is all commercial equipment, but since we've gone this far on the assumption that you want to make it all, let's look at a string.

Like everything else, strings have been made of almost anything the archer could put his hands on. Time and chemistry have changed the list considerably—time limiting it and chemistry adding to it.

Today you will want to use either linen—the old standby—or one of the new synthetics: fortisan or dacron. There's much to be said for any one of the three materials; only time and shooting can tell you which one you prefer. But making a string with one of them is the same as with the others.

String making is difficult to describe. All the reading in the world won't give you as much information as five or ten minutes of watching.

How to Make Bowstrings

But for the moment we'll have to be content with trying to describe the process as lucidly as possible.

The materials you need for making the string are simple. They are the same for either a two-strand or a three-strand string. From personal experience we prefer the two-strand type, but that may be because it is simpler and can be made speedily and under the most adverse conditions in the field. Basically you need two nails, a cake of wax, a knife and your string, no matter what its composition. Anything you may add to this list, as for instance a string board, is nothing but an extra bit of luxury. When we've finished with a description of actual string making we'll go into the matter of string boards. But for the moment, just pretend that you're way out in the open with the bare essentials we've already listed. Just as a note of interest: wax, when an archer speaks of it, is beeswax—either pure or mixed. To mix, use three parts of beeswax with one part resin, while liquid. The resultant mixture adds to the sticking quality of the pure wax.

Getting back to our basic string. There are two types of strings in use today—one with double loops and one with a loop at one end and a knot at the other. The double loop is, for my taste, neater, just as serviceable and just as easy to make and use. On the other hand, thousands of archers adhere to the single loop string, since the knot at the bottom, being adjustable, permits of more change, should the string be too long or too short. So we'll start with the single loop, double-strand string.

On any flat or semi-flat surface mark out the distance of the bowstring you want, plus 5 in. Drive your two nails into the marks, then tie one end of your cord to one of the nails.

If you should choose linen, get what is called Barbour's No. 12. It comes in a ball and should, if possible, be encased in a box, with the inside end drawn through a hole in the cover. While this isn't ab-

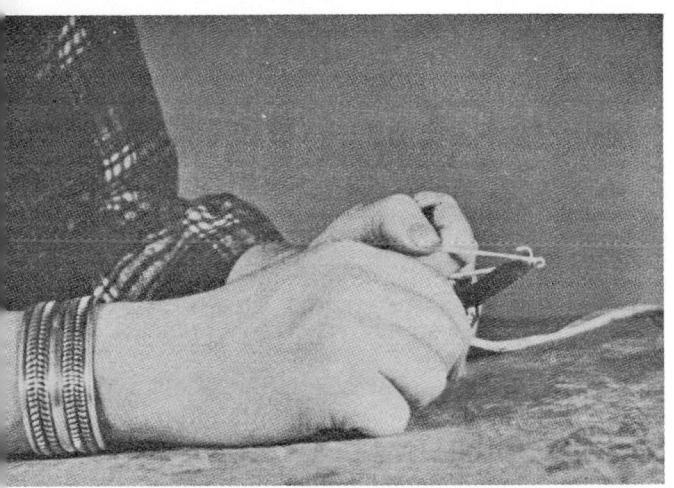

After looping thread around two nails spread right distance apart, lift off one end of loop and cut through to make two strands.

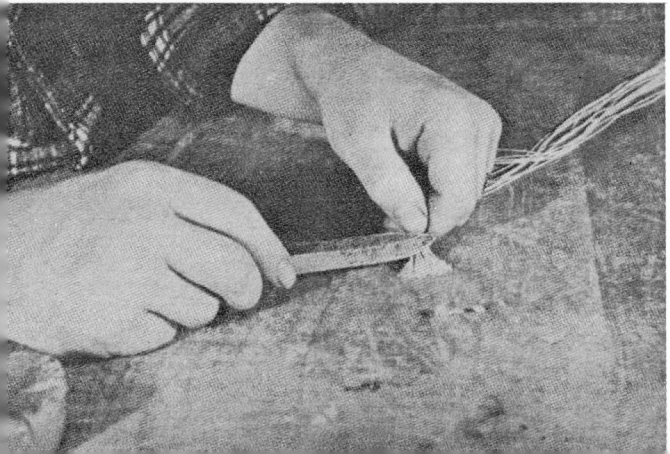

Shave ends of each strand gently by holding knife blade flat against them and give feather-cut to the tip. Be sure knife is very sharp.

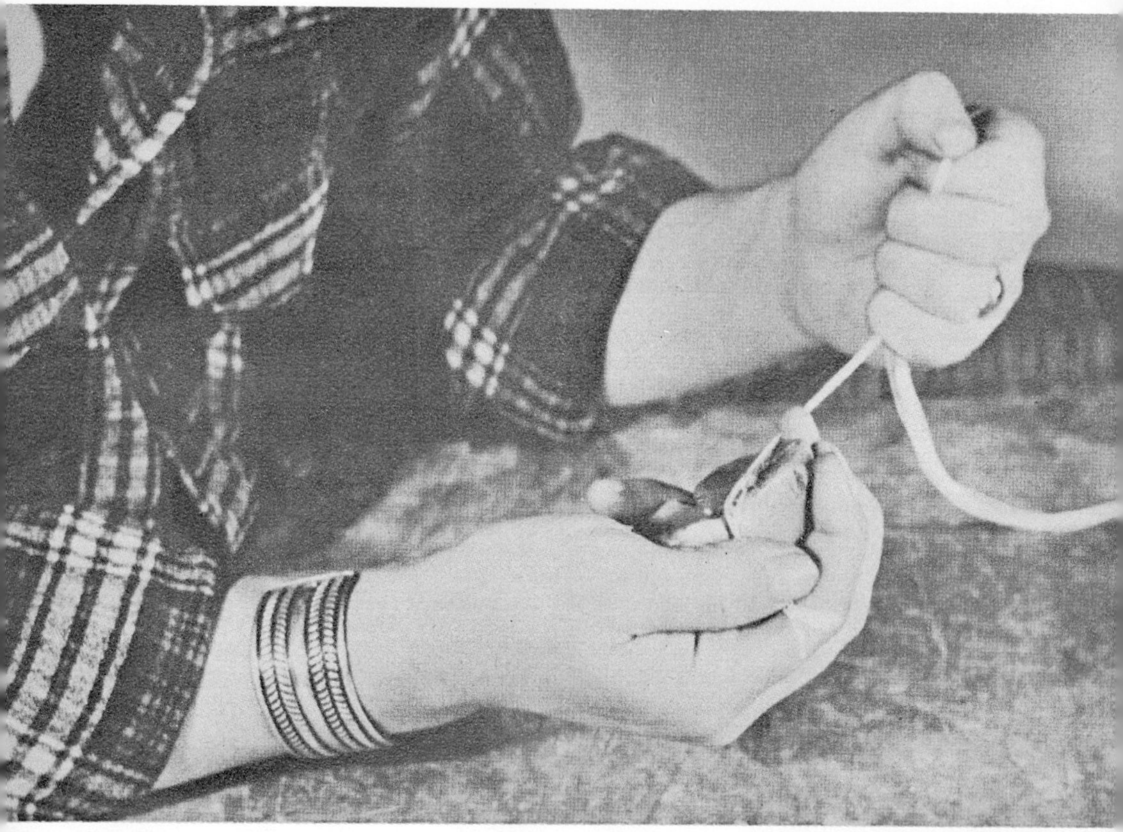

solutely necessary, it'll save you yards and yards of rat's nests when you come to the end of the ball. In the field an envelope with the ball in it will serve the trick nicely.

Having tied the one end, begin to make loops from that nail to the other and back, taking care that the cord lies as smoothly as possible. The surface over which you're working may not be perfectly flat—in the field it's often an old log—so take care not to snag any of your loops. Keep the tension equal all the way around, but don't attempt to draw the string too tight.

When you've made enough turns, tie the ball end of the cord to the free end, which was fastened to the first nail. The number of strands you'll use will depend on two factors—the weight, or draw of your bow, and the tensile strength of your string material. A good rule of thumb with Barbour's No. 12 is thirty-six strands for a bow with a pull of fifty pounds. The synthetics, being stronger, don't require as many strands for bows of equal weight.

Since this is to be a double strand string, you will have made seventy-two turns, so that thirty-six single strands lie on each

Now wax the two shaved ends thoroughly as shown to achieve a taper: wax strands firmly.

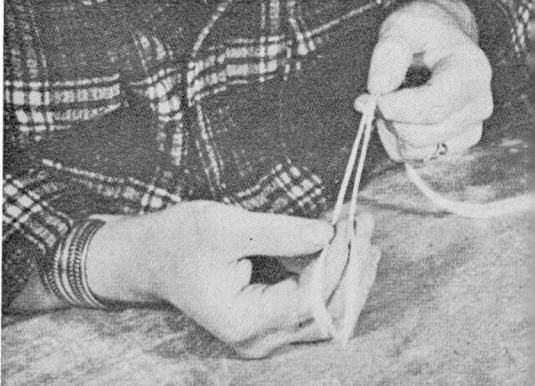

After repeating same process with other end of looped string, separate ends between your fingers.

how to make bowstrings

side of the nails. Your next step will be to wax the string thoroughly, to within 6 in. of the nails. This serves to hold the separate strands together. Then slip the loop off one of the nails and cut through with your knife, being sure to sever every one of the doubled threads.

Lay the two ends, matched for length, against some level surface and with the flat edge of the knife, tease them out toward the open end. Shave them gently, giving a feather cut to the last bit. Be sure that the blade of the knife is good and sharp, since a good taper can only be gotten in this way. When you have enough taper (and the actual loss in length should be just a fraction of an inch) wax the two strands thoroughly, and continue the waxing down to the point where you stopped before. Repeat this with the other end of the string.

At this point you should have a long, well-waxed strand which splits into two equal parts at either end. There should be no kinking or twisting, other than a certain amount which you may have imparted in the waxing. One thing to watch carefully is that there are no uneven areas: in other words, you made sure before cutting that no single strand was bearing more than its share of weight.

Take one end of the string and hold it between the thumb and forefinger of the

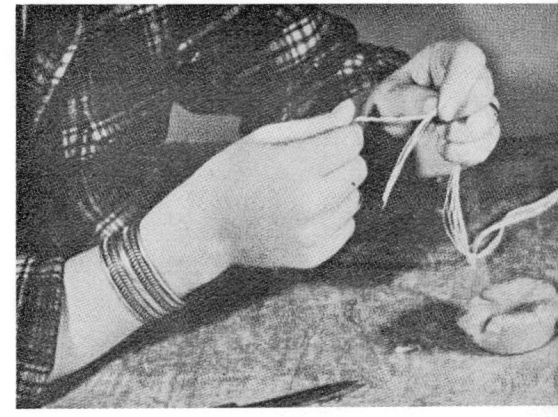

Next twist each loose strand between thumb and forefinger to shape taper. Twist away from center.

Turn twisted strand down under untwisted one and keep twisting, now alternately one after the other.

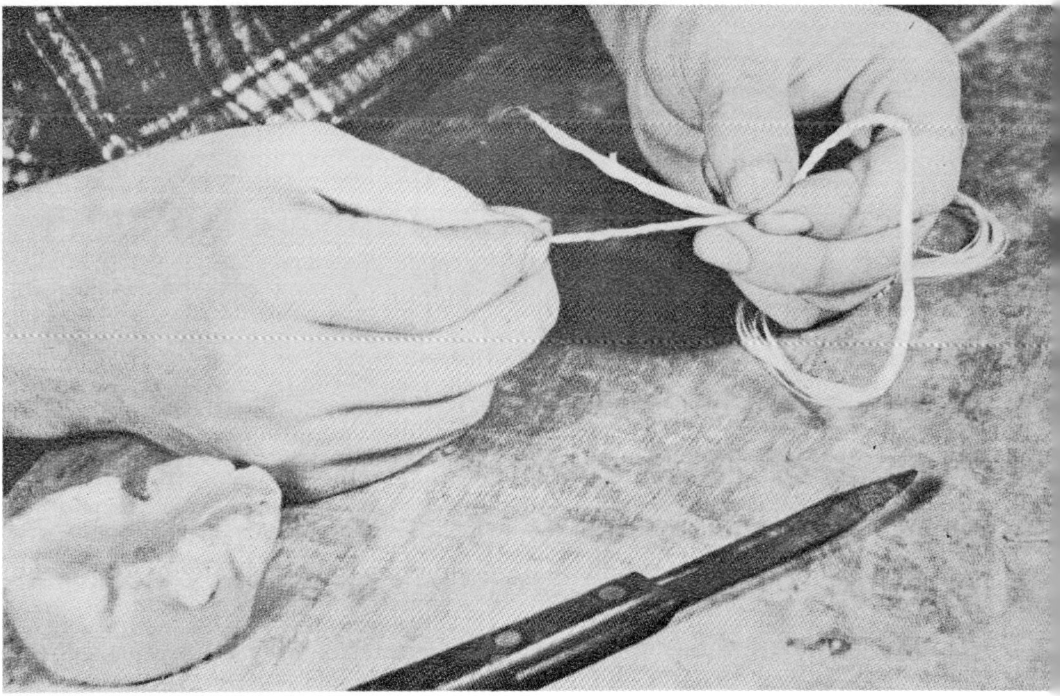

43

Soon a rope-like effect will appear. Hold strands separate as shown, while you twist at free end.

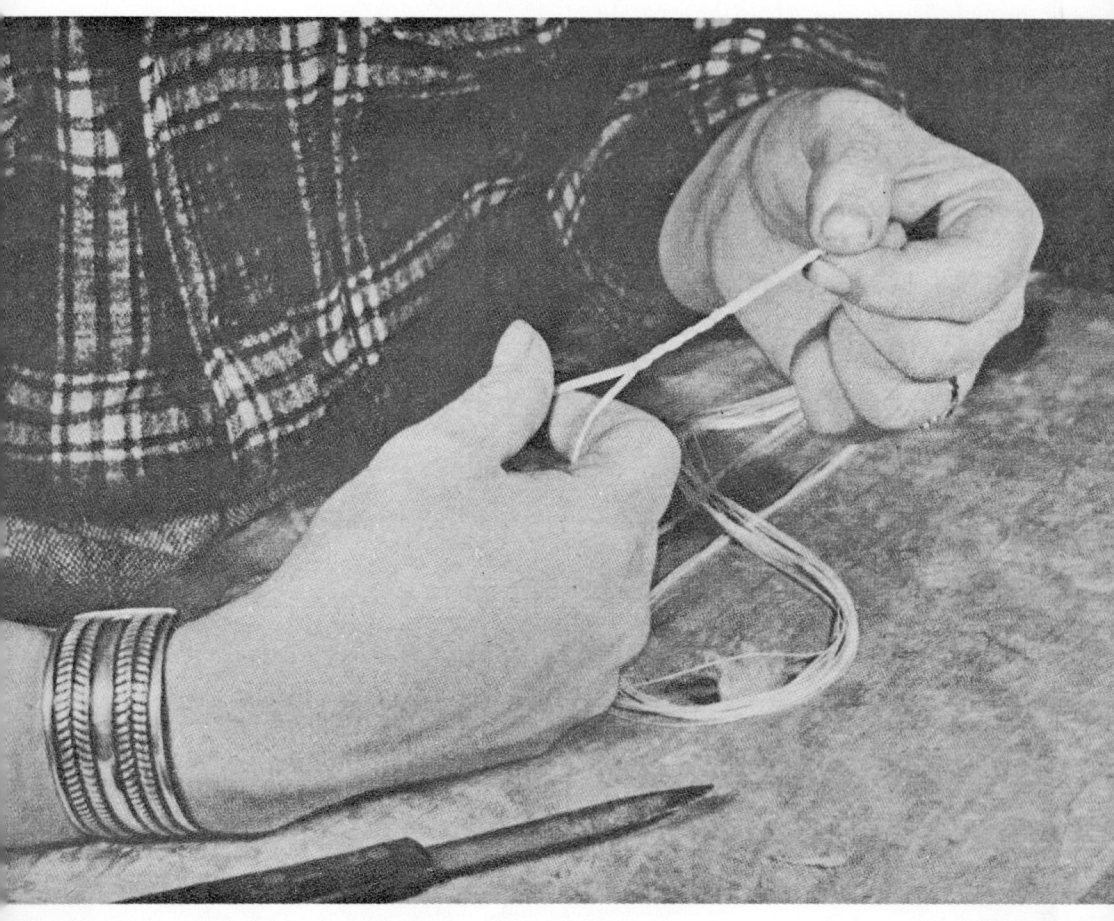

left hand about five inches from the end. With your right hand, separate the two strand ends so that they are one above the other. Take the top strand and twist it away from you with the thumb and finger of the right hand, at the same time bringing it down and around toward you. You set a twist that is opposite to the turn of the actual string. Keep the pressure constant—not too tight and yet not loose, as you continue this move, spinning and turning the two strands alternately. As you work on you'll see that you are gradually building up a neat little rope. When the rope is about three inches long loop it over your hand and begin to work it back into the main strands.

To do this you will have to separate the two parts of the main strand. It will be simple, in spite of the wax, since you already have the split started, in your hand. Don't attempt to take the split more than a foot down without seeing to it that the two parts don't ravel and kink. Follow the length of the string ending with two long strands, joined in your hand by a short length of rope.

In the meantime, don't let the rope undo itself. When you've finished the split, bring the short ends of your rope loop around and lay them against the two long strands. They need not be paired. Then go back to your twist and counter turn, keeping the short ends close to the main strands, using wax if you feel that the work is slipping. The two ends, which were tapered by the shaving you gave them with the knife blade, will gradually work themselves down into the two main strands and you will find a rope loop in your hand, about

how TO MAKE BOWSTRINGS

When the rope-like twist is about 5 in. long, you are ready to form the loop to fit bow-nock.

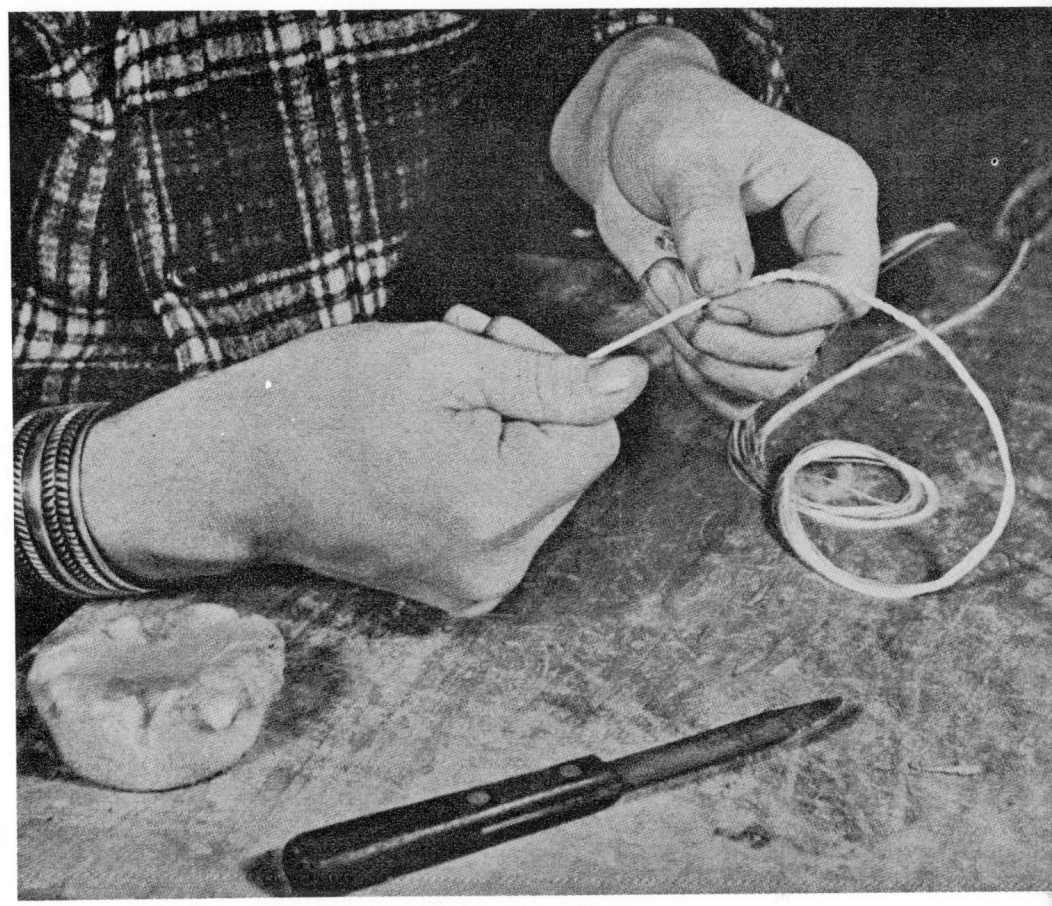

2½ in. deep. This loop will set in the upper nock of your bow.

Now, twisting with the turn of your loop, work your way down the length of the string. Hook the loop over one of your nails for this step since you'll need all the reach you can get and both hands are going to be busy.

Six inches from the other end, take the main strand in your left hand and the two open ends in your right. Begin the same process you used in making the loop at the other end, twisting out and turning in, keeping your stress constant, and waxing as you go. At this end the taper will work itself into a thin end, which is well twisted and ropelike.

The string is now finished, except for the serving. Put a timber hitch in the straight end and slide the loop itself down over the upper nock of your bow. Set the timber hitch and brace the bow. Since the timber hitch is completely adjustable, it is easy to get a proper fistmele in stringing. A fistmele, is, by definition, the distance between the belly of the bow, at the grip, and the string. Usually it is measured by putting the fist against the belly with the thumb extended. This was the classical method of determining the fistmele, but today we use an approximate measure of six inches. Once your fistmele is set, you are ready to serve the string.

Serving protects the string, wherever the most wear and tear will take effect. The three points to watch are the two bow nocks and the point on the string where the arrow nock is placed, the nocking point. Since this is a permanent point, the wear on the string at this point is the worst. With

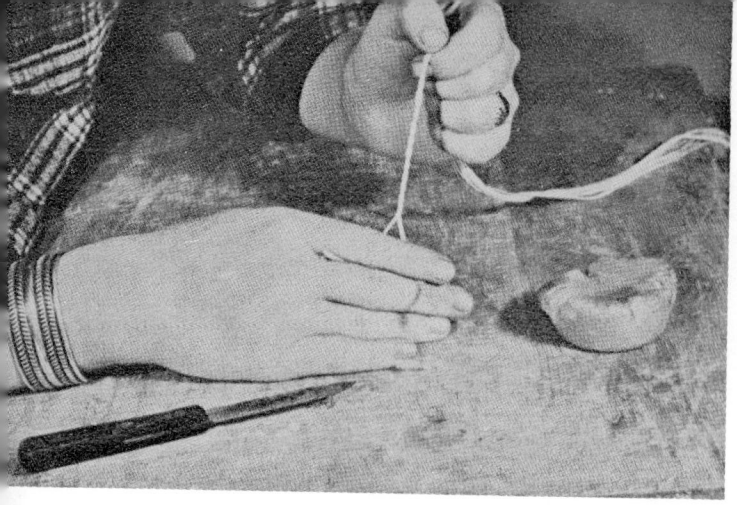

First step in making loop: separate two strands at end of twist for a distance of little more than 1½ in. Wax will keep the threads stiff.

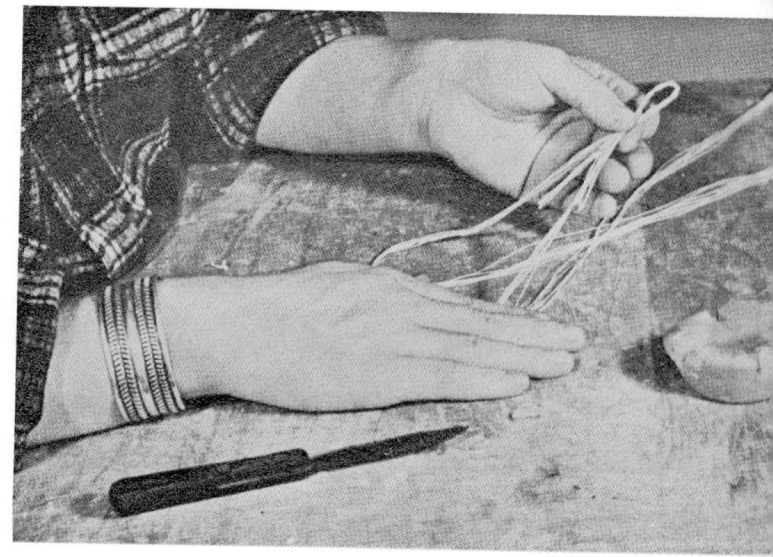

Now bend rope-twisted end around as shown to form a loop, holding loop-base in position where strands separate, with thumb, finger.

the strung bow in hand take an arrow and set it against the string in the proper position—against the arrow plate and with the nock firmly against the string. Mark this point on the string and remove the arrow. Using this as a starting point, make another mark 2 in. above it on the string and a third 3 in. below. This 5-in. section of your string will have to be served.

Serving by hand is tedious. Today, few of us do it; we depend on mechanical servers. Others have put their faith in specially made tapes, which are supposed to fill the same function as a string serving. However, serving is not difficult—only time consuming. The material for serving can be almost any stout thread—even a strand of the stuff you used for the actual string will do in a pinch. But a good safe bet is Cuttyhunk, although surgical silk is another prime favorite. Start winding the serving around your string, from the mark above the nocking point. Keep the pressure even and see to it that the loops lie tight against one another. Don't put on too much pressure, since it will cut the strands of the bowstring beneath and completely defeat your purpose in serving.

When you come to the lower mark, tie off the thread by laying eight loose loops below the actual serving. Bring the end of the serving thread back through the loose loops and cut it flush to the serving. Rub the entire serving with a tiny amount of shellac, let dry and repeat. The second time, add a little oil to the shellac and rub

How to Make Bowstrings

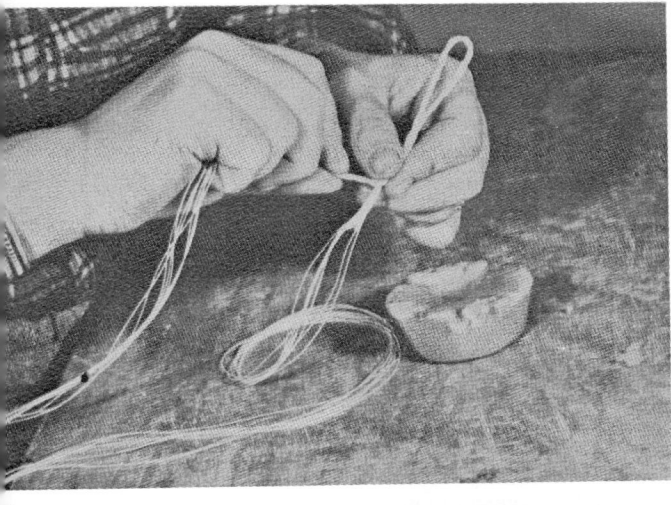

Weave free ends of strands into corresponding sections of main string, which have not been made into a rope but are also separate down their length. Then, taking one of these, twist around base of loop as shown in photo. Be careful not to snarl main strands.

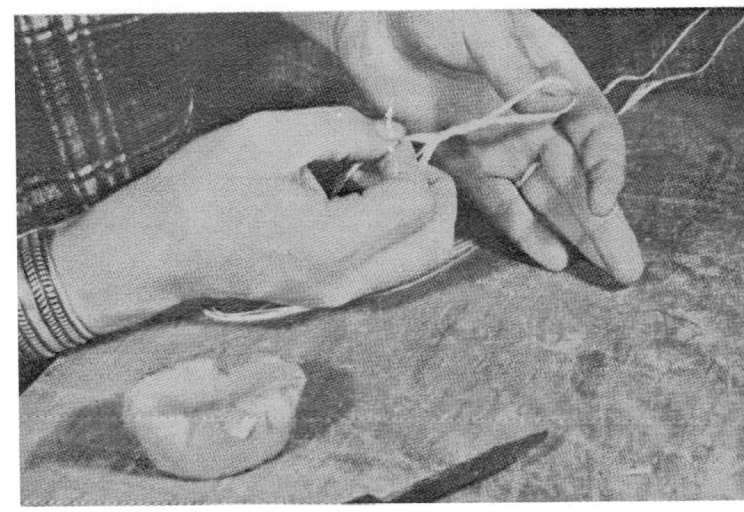

Now with thumb in loop, make a few twists: but hold two main strands apart with finger, to prevent snarling of the strands, which must be loose.

it dry. Finish by rubbing the serving with paraffin or candle wax, which will let your fingers slide easily off the string.

The final stage is to wax—with beeswax—the string on the bow and then, with a piece of old soft leather, rub it freely up and down its length. The heat of the friction will melt the wax just enough to penetrate every fiber and at the same time you are rounding the string through the leather. It's a good plan, too, to leather-rub and wax the string before you lay on the serving, as well as afterward.

And that makes your first bowstring.

The only difference in making a double-loop string, as against the one just described is in the latter stage. When you've completed the first loop and have separated the two main strands, do it over again at the other end, taking care that your twist runs the same, so that the two ends aren't fighting one another. Serving is the same with any string, except that in certain cases you may wish to serve the string from the loop down onto the main body for an inch or so. This is only necessary where the nock of the bow is rough (and it never should be) causing extra pressure on those sections of the string.

A three-strand string, either single or double loop is more complicated. Made with reinforcement, it relieves the necessity for serving the loops. To make such a string, let's go back to our original two nails, stuck in our flat surface, only this time shorten the distance to one inch over

47

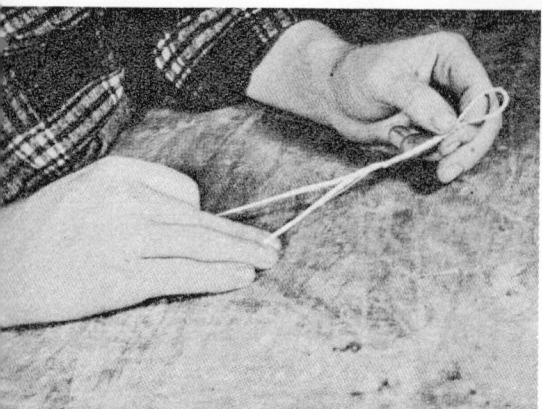

Closeup view at left shows completed loop. It will be strong enough to withstand the pull of bow.

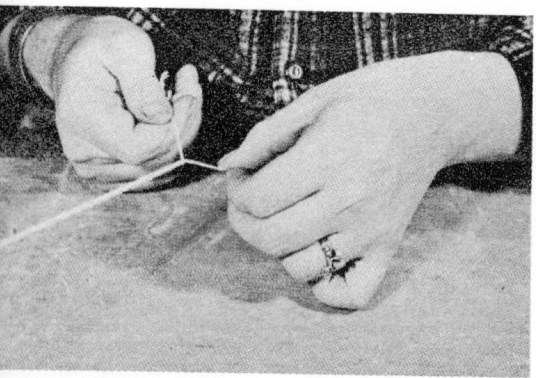

To weave taper in opposite end of string, anchor loop on nail and twist free strands into rope.

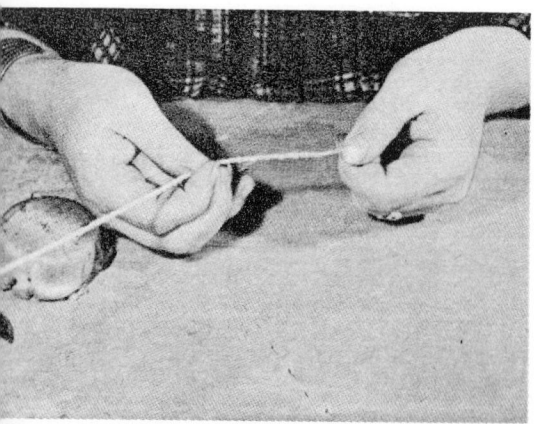

Twirl the ends of rope together to form taper, adding additional beeswax to hold shape, if needed.

the total of the desired finished length.

Again, tie one end of the ball of cord to a nail. Go around the other nail, making the usual loops, only this time, stop after you've made six complete turns, which will give you twelve strands. Tie the two ends of the string and remove from the nails. Wax the six double strands thoroughly, cut the ends and taper in turn, as in the first string. Then lay this strand to one side and repeat twice more. Now you have three strands, of twelve threads each, well waxed and tapered. Your last step here is to make one more strand, only this time it will be only half as thick, three threads to a side instead of six. Remove it, wax and cut into six equal lengths. Taper each of these six short strands carefully and put them aside, with the three main strands.

Take one of the main strands and lay one of the short strands against it. Work the two into one another as carefully as you can, leaving about an inch of the short end running beyond the main strand. The wax, which you've already applied will hold the two together. Repeat this with the second and third long strands so that you have three reinforced long strands.

This time when you take the strands in your left hand, you'll have three to deal with. Grip them 8 or 9 in. from the end and roll away as you bring the top one toward you. It'll be easiest for you if you anchor them in turn under your left thumb. When you've made about 3 in. of rope, turn them back on the main strands, forming a loop. Match the short end, farthest from you with the main strand farthest away and blend them together, using a spin away from you and working them even closer with the wax. Be sure that the short ends are free of any kinks. Match the other two strands the same way and work down into the main strands so that the short ends, with their tapers are gradually worked into the main string.

Hang your newly completed loop over a nail and tie with a short end of string to keep the rope from untwisting while you work on the other end.

Pull the main strands free, with equal pressure and work in the three short ends

how TO MAKE BOWSTRINGS

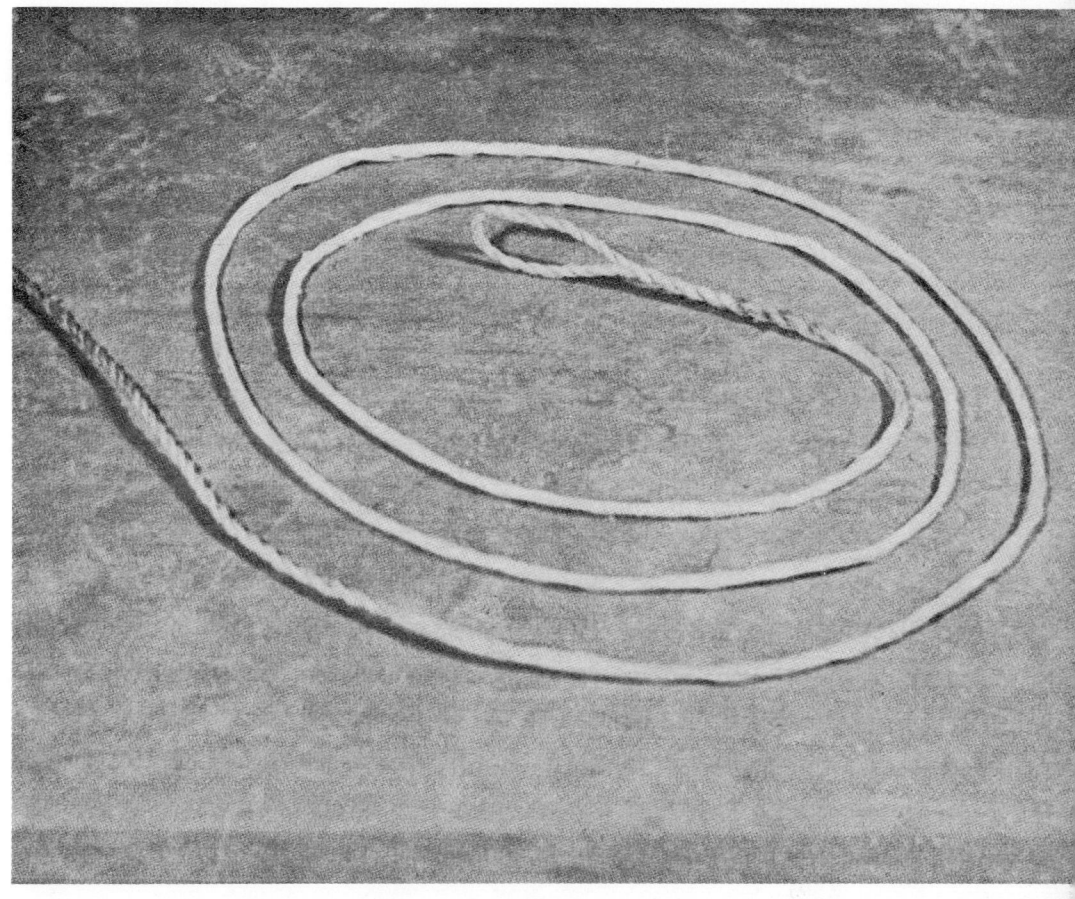

Completed single-loop bowstring is shown here: main body of string is not tightly twisted into rope as are ends. To make a double-loop string, merely repeat looping process at both ends.

that you've saved. This gives you the same reinforced main strands, just as in the upper end of the string. The next step is up to you—a choice between the tapered strand, which you can use on the bottom of the bow as a timber hitch, or a double-loop. Twist the main string, in either case, waxing as you twist and shape with leather. Serve and you have a three-strand bowstring.

If you intend to make any strings it may be well to make a string board. The simplest one has one fixed nail and a second that is adjustable to suit the length of the string you want to make. You can set one nail and at the other end of your working area drill a series of holes 1 in. apart. The second nail can be moved into any of these at will. It's a very handy tool for field use.

When you go out to shoot, always take a spare string or so along. The best stringmaker can't guarantee the life of a string and you may not have time to sit down and make one, once you're out. It may take only a half hour but that thirty-minute period may mean the difference between a big buck or none at all. So, when you make a string for your bow, make two others at the same time. They'll keep well under almost any conditions and they take up almost no room, either in a pocket of your quiver, or in a tackle case. •

49

The best commercial arrows are made by hand. Here, girl is trimming feathers of arrows held in clamps.

Arrows and Arrow Making

The dyed-in-the-wool archer makes his own arrows to be certain of their trueness, but even the amateur can achieve accurate results with practice.

NOW that you have your bow, you're going to want arrows. And at this point it's only fair to say that the making of arrows is more difficult than the making of a bow. As someone once said, "A good arrow isn't too hard to make, but getting twelve of them alike, is something else again."

Before we go into the details of construction, let's examine the arrow and its parts. Each arrow is divided into three parts—the shaftment, the shaft itself, or stele, and the foreshaft. Roughly the

Photo by Hal Kelly, courtesy
Robin Hood Archery Co.

three parts divide the arrow equally, the shaftment includes the nock, the feathers and the crest; the stele is plain and the foreshaft contains the pile or head and the footing, if any.

Footed arrows are those with some form of reinforcement toward the pile or head. Since the greatest strain on the arrow occurs in this area, archers often splice heavier, harder woods there, to prevent breakage. Arrows that do not have footing are called "self arrows."

Most modern arrows are made of Port Orford Cedar, and through the course of time this wood has been found to be the best for arrow making. However, very serviceable arrows can be made from other woods, which include Norway Pine, Douglas Fir and birch. The last is one of the best woods for hunting and roving arrows, which must take a terrific amount of knocking around in the field. It does not make an arrow fly quite as true as Port Orford Cedar, but in the long run it is a good wood, especially for practice work. It is the wood used in arrows which you see on the archery shooting ranges. Birch is seldom if ever footed.

The easiest way to start your arrow making is to buy a bunch of birch dowels. Get the $\frac{5}{16}$ in. diameter kind and try to select those which are straight, without knots or cross-graining. If you are unable to make a selection before purchasing, sort out the dowels afterward and straighten those which are simply bent, by means of steaming, or holding over a hot plate.

If you insist on doing everything by hand, you can, of course, buy strips of birch that are $\frac{5}{16}$ in. square and round the dowels with a plane and sandpaper. However, since the hard part is yet to come, I'd advise you to save your energies for the later, more difficult stages.

Either way, you should now have before you a dozen birch dowels, as straight as you can get them. You will remember how to select the proper arrow length for yourself (see the chapter on "Selection of Equipment") and the next thing is to cut the dozen dowels so that they are all exactly that length.

Your next move will be to put piles on the twelve arrows. One of the simplest and easiest of all practice piles is the 150 grain metal

Clamped hunting arrows being trimmed in large manufacturing plant make an unusually impressive sight.

Courtesy Ben Pearson

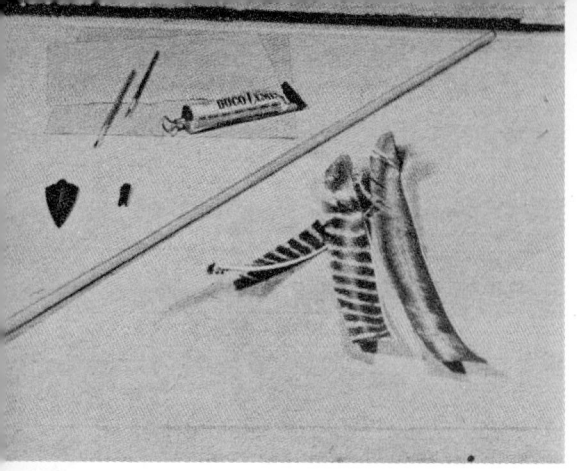

Equipment needed to make arrows is simple: some Duco cement, turkey feathers, points, birch dowels

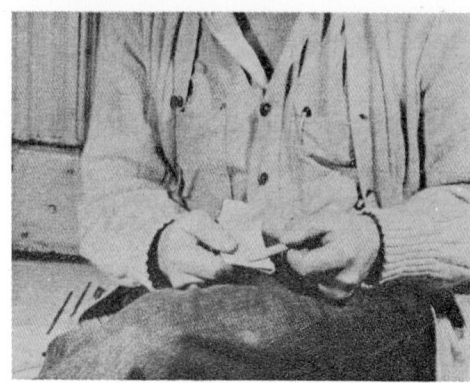

To attach point, first sand dowel-end until it is peg-shaped. It should fit snugly into point-jacket.

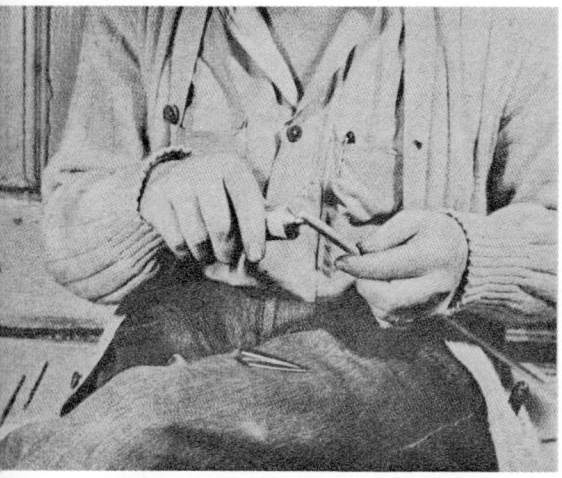

Next, cover dowel-end with smooth thin coating of cement and allow to dry. Do same with point-jacket.

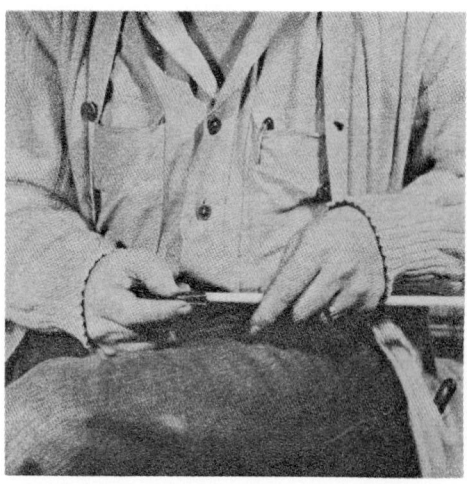

Fit point onto dowel as snugly as possible and use a prick punch on jacket-sides to imbed metal in wood.

bullet jacket. These can be purchased from an archery supply dealer, or from many other sources. For a perfectly blunt head, which will not only serve for practice but will be excellent on small game, the cut off cases of .30 and .32 caliber shells will fit your arrows nicely. With the 150 grain metal bullet jacket, you need to take a wood file and round the ends of your arrows down so that they fit into the jacket very snugly. Drive the jacket well onto the end of the arrow and using a prick punch, anchor it into the wood. Actually, this will hold better than glue in the majority of cases.

However, if you don't trust that method you can drill a small hole completely through the jacket and the wood. I'd suggest you use a hole of $\frac{1}{16}$ in. diameter. Drive a brad through the hole, cut off at either side and file flush. In either case you should by now have twelve arrows with heads.

Practice piles are the easiest to make but broadheads are not too difficult. They, naturally, are used only for hunting—since their construction makes them useless in practice. If you plan to hunt and want to get used to the heft and proportion of the hunting arrows you can weight your practice heads with lead until the arrow comes to the same total weight and balance as your hunting shafts.

Hunting heads are made for penetration. Whereas a bullet kills by shock, the arrow kills by entering and cutting. Game may travel after being hit with an arrow, but the chances are, with any good hit, that they won't travel far, particularly if you follow sensible rules in going after a hurt animal. The broadhead will stop an animal

Arrows and Arrow Making

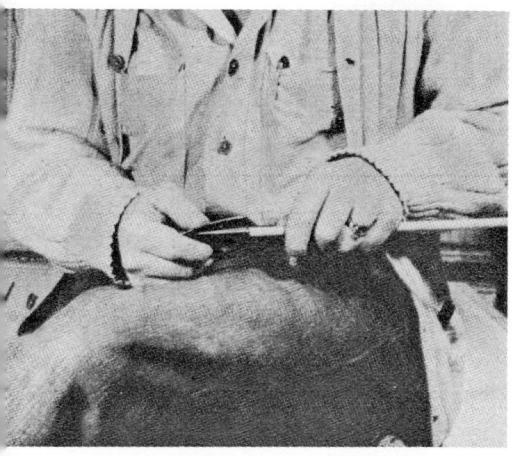

Another way to anchor point or head is by drilling 1/16-in. hole through jacket and dowel, then rivet.

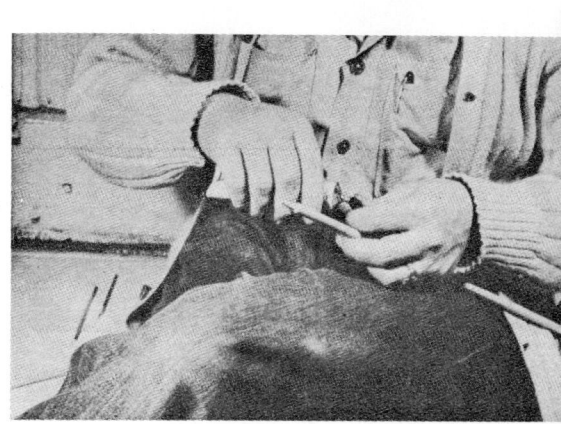

This photo shows another type of pegged end: here, jacket of head or point fits flush with the wood.

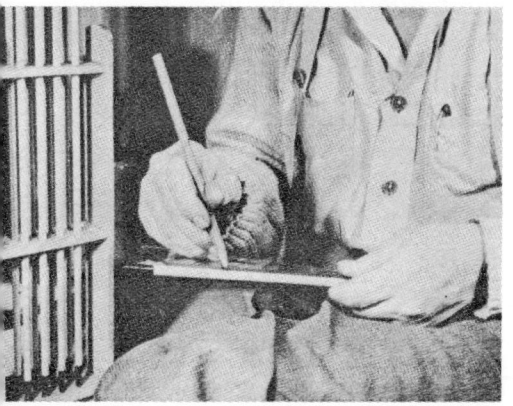

To attach feathers, first draw position-lines on dowel, using a drafting triangle for trueness.

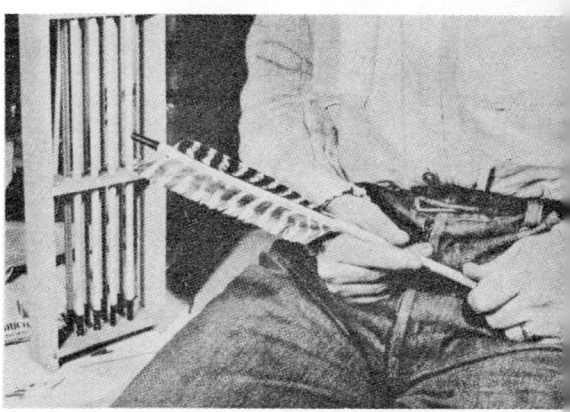

Cock feather should be different color and must be glued on dowel exactly at right angle to nock.

for the simple reason that it will bleed the animal to death.

Our broadheads then must be so made as to yield maximum penetration and maximum cutting. To date, steel has been the best popular material for hunting heads. If you have the time and patience to chip flint arrowheads, Dr. Pope has proved that the natural fluting along the edge of a flint head greatly increases the penetrating quality of the arrow. Today, to the best of my knowledge, there is only one man in the United States chipping flint heads: Jim Ramsey, of Lincoln, New Mexico. He turns out such beautiful heads that one is tempted to use them for display rather than hunting. Write to him for information or purchase prices.

The best material for the steel head is spring steel, $\frac{1}{32}$ in. thick, in strips of 1-in. width. For smaller heads, old power hacksaw blades give you a good enough grade of steel, but in general it's preferable to use strip steel which is inexpensive.

The shape of the broadhead is roughly that of a triangle, or a foreshortened diamond. In some instances the after-edges of the triangle are countersunk, giving deep barbs.

The barbs are actually superfluous, and if they are offensive to you, they can be eliminated in making the head, by modification to the form of a pointed tear-drop. The best method is to choose a form which you like and make a template, or pattern, in that exact form—which can be used over and over again. A good over-all size, suitable for most game will be 2½ in. long and just a shade under 1 in. wide, at the point immediately above the barbs.

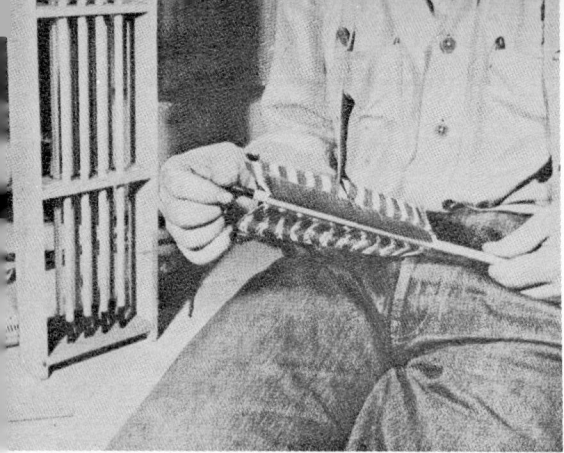
After cock feather is in place, other feathers are attached: all are spaced 120 degrees apart.

When glue on feathers is thoroughly set, the next phase is trimming: cut cardboard strips to shape.

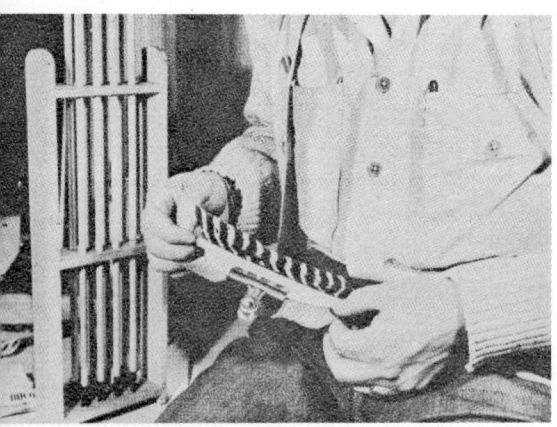
Attach cardboard templates to feathers with a clamp-type paper clip as shown here in photograph.

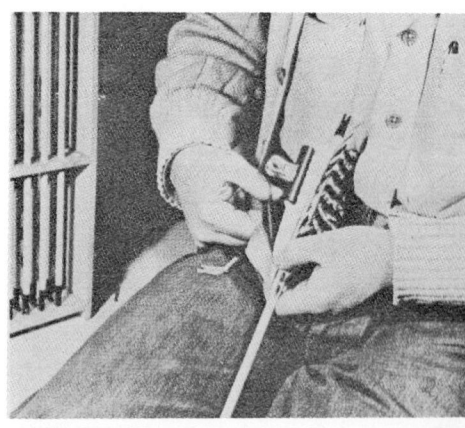
Then, using extra sharp manicuring scissors, cut along cardboard edges to trim away excess feather.

A second form of the broadhead is made with a tang, or tongue, which is held in a slot in the arrow. If you choose this form of head, be sure that your template has a tang at least 1 in. long and of the same breadth as the diameter of your arrow.

The simple, or untanged, head should have its barbs, or modifications, formed by filing a semi-circle out of the base of the strip. Working toward the point, from the deepest spot on the semicircle, drill a $\frac{1}{16}$ in. hole ¼ in. from the back edge.

The cutting edge, on both types, is set up by cutting a bevel on both sides of the leading edge. Make the bevel at least ⅛ in. wide, since it's impossible to keep a good cutting edge with a narrower slant.

Cut your heads in batches of a dozen or more at a time. Using the template, scribe the outlines on the long steel strips with a hard point. You then saw the rough heads out of the strip, in a vise, or if you wish you can break them out with a hammer. If you are making the tanged heads, you'll have to stick to the hacksaw method. In either case, if your steel seems to be too brittle, you can anneal (or soften) the metal by heating it to a cherry red and then letting it cool slowly, in air.

Working from the rough shapes, you now file or grind to the marks that you scribed from the template. Next cut the semicircle, drill the hole and grind the bevel to a rough edge. Be careful in grinding, since the friction sets up more than enough heat to burn your fingers severely. Keep both the grinding surface and the arrowhead as wet as possible.

The head must now be tempered to a

ARROWS AND ARROW MAKING

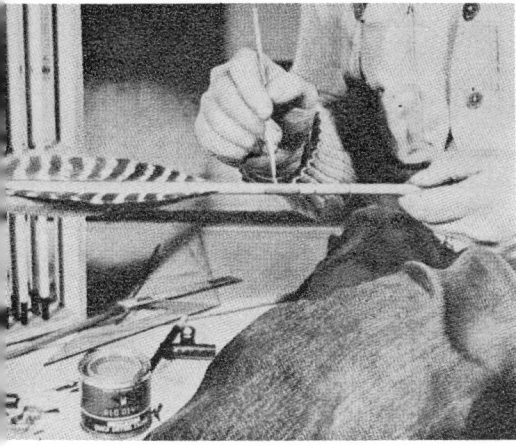

Most archers decorate their arrows, both for the colorful effect and for identification in the field.

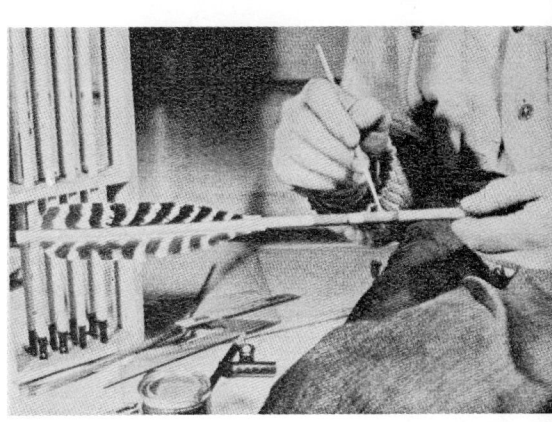

Color combinations are personal matter. Hold brush steady and twirl arrow so paint runs on evenly.

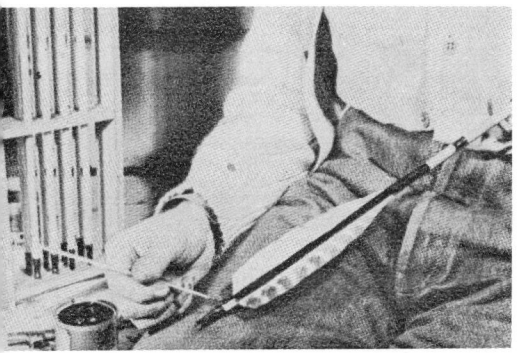

Hunting or field arrows are often colored all the way up to nock: they are easier to follow in woods.

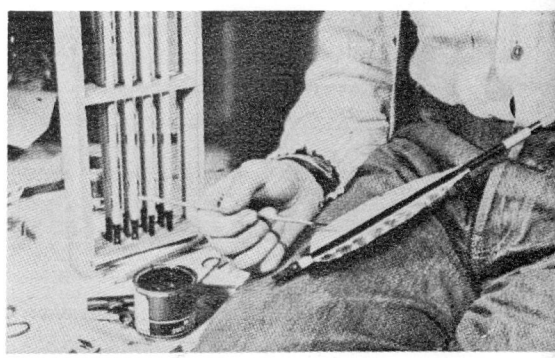

If paint slips onto feather-ribs be sure to remove it with solvent or it might spoil trueness of spin. Below is shown a finished hunting arrow with a broadhead point. Feathers are longer on this type.

tough resiliency. The finished product must not be soft—since then it won't hold an edge, nor can it be too brittle, or it will chip and break. First heat the head until it is again a bright red and toss it instantly into cold water. The metal is now glass-hard and can be brought to a beautiful polish. The next step is to reheat the head, this time as slowly and evenly as possible, using a low flame. As the metal heats you'll see a range of color changes—gold, yellow blue, dark blue and then pale blue. As the head reaches the deep blue, toss it into cold water again. The dark blue will remain on the surface and serves the extra purpose of not reflecting light easily, which will be a help when you come to actual hunting.

The easiest way to fix the broadhead on the arrow is to use the bullet jacket pile,

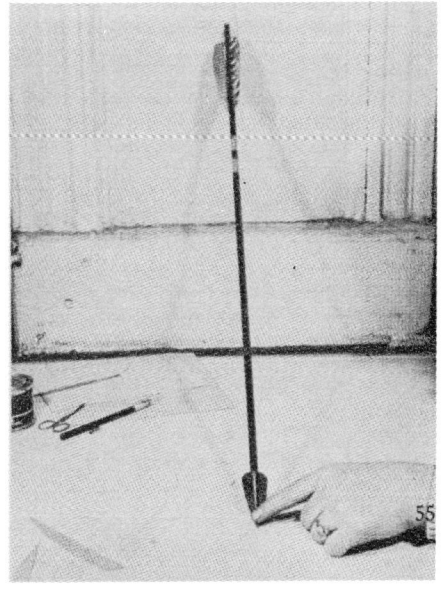

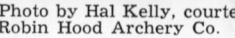
Photo by Hal Kelly, courtesy Robin Hood Archery Co.

Arrow dowels are usually of a 5/16-in. diameter; best woods are Port Orford Cedar, Norway Pine, Douglas Fir, birch.

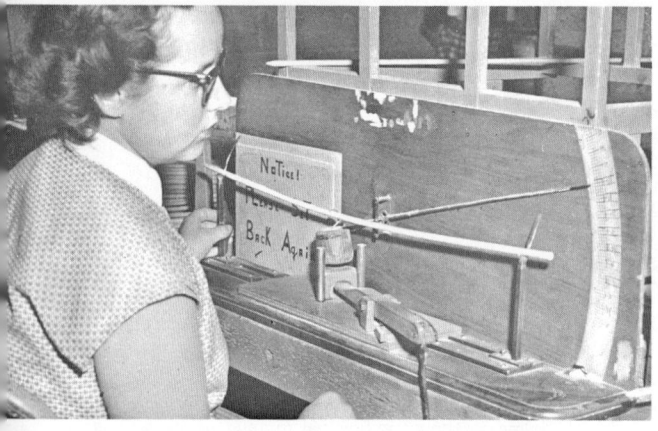

Commercial arrow makers always check stiffness of dowels in a special type instrument to be sure of firm shafts.

Courtesy Bear Archery Co.

we spoke of before. Flatten the end of the tip, just enough to allow you to make a saw cut. Make the cut with a saw blade of the same thickness as your broadhead and be sure that the cut is even on both sides so that the head will sit true in the slot. Drill a $\frac{1}{16}$ in. hole through the jacket and the wood, so that it coincides with the hole you've previously bored in the head. Seat the head in the saw-cut, run a rivet from side to side and round off the heads of the rivet as smoothly as you can. The single rivet will hold the head as securely as you'll ever need, particularly if you've seated the bullet jacket properly, in the beginning. Another way to set the head in place is to cut the jacket, as above, and then solder the blade into position. It gives you an even, more solid head, but it requires a very fine hand with a soldering iron.

In setting the tanged heads there are two workable methods. One involves the use of a fine wire wrapping and the other uses a thin metal sleeve. The latter is easier and gives you a neater looking finished job. Slot the end of your arrow, along the plane of the nock, so that the end of the wood completely covers the tang and extends up onto the actual blade for half an inch. The wood should be rounded down so that it meets the blade without any abrupt edge. Remove the head from the slot and slip a sleeve of metal tubing over the end of the shaft. Replace the blade, and holding it in position, bore two holes in the sleeve, through which you may drive $\frac{1}{16}$ in. rivets, to hold the assembly.

The wrapping method serves the same effect. The wood is slotted and rounded and a small hole is drilled through the wood

Arrow shafts are also weighed in order to determine distribution of weight: a well balanced arrow is very accurate.

Courtesy Bear Archery Co.

Closeup of commercial fletching device showing how arrows are clamped in place by nock-ends so feathering is easy.

Photo by Hal Kelly, courtesy Robin Hood Archery Co.

an ⅛ in., more or less, below the bottom of the saw cut. The blade is inserted and fine steel wire is wrapped around the shaft as tightly as possible. Start the winding at the head and work toward the nock. When you come to the hole, run your wire through and break it off on the other side. It's a good plan to finish the job with a line of solder to prevent the wire from slipping out of the hole, and to make the whole wrapping permanent. Unfortunately, this way of setting the tangs gives you a heavy and cumbersome head, which must be compensated for when you come to put the feathers on.

You now turn to the other end and work on the nocks. This nock, like the nock on the bow, is for the string and there are dozens of ways of making it. The simplest way is to make a cut in the end of the arrow, *across the grain*. The cut should be ¼ in. deep and roughly ⅛ in. wide. If you can, make the cut with three hack saw blades bound together. Or make two cuts with one blade and clean the area carefully with a knife. The edge and bottom of the nock are then sanded smooth, to complete the step.

If you feel that your arrows are going to take a lot of beating you might consider the plastic nock. Inexpensive, and obtainable from almost every archery dealer, they are easy to apply, come in varying colors and can be changed in minutes. They are cast—in other words, mass produced—from a material similar to celluloid. The hole in the base is tapered to accommodate varying arrow diameters. To set a plastic nock, use a cellulose-based plastic glue. The entire operation is completed in a very

Another method of feather-trimming is burning: it is usually done by electrically heated wire.

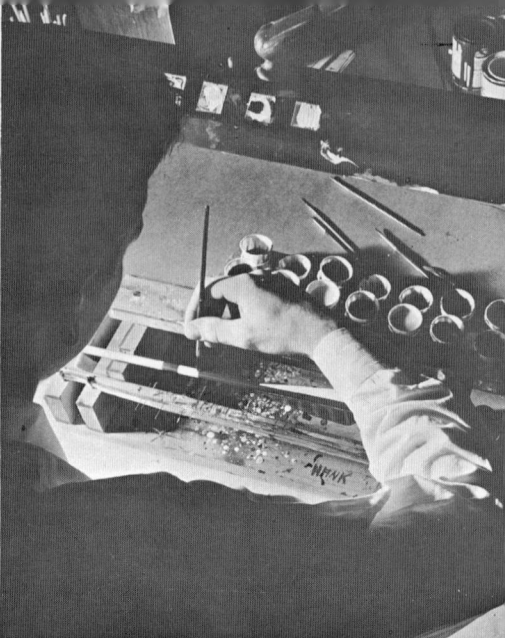

Professional arrow decorators use a lathe-like device to turn shaft, which speeds up the process.

short time. If one becomes broken, you hold a match to it and it burns off, leaving the wood unharmed. Plastic nocks have another feature that is a great boon to the hunter and field archer. The nocks made for hunting arrows have a little ridge or nob cast in at the cock feather position so that the shooter need not remove his eye from the target to tell if the arrow is in proper position on the string.

Some people, however, prefer to make all the equipment themselves. For them, nock reinforcements to toughen a plain slot nock come in the form of wood and fiber wedges, or sheets. The latter is simpler—a slot is sawed in the wood, this time with the grain, and a sheet of fiber is glued into place in the slot and then trimmed flush. You then cut your nock, across the grain—as in the basic method—and your reinforcement is done. A slightly fancier version calls for a wedge insertion, instead of the flat sheet. Again, fiber is the best material from the standpoint of practicality, but horn wedges set in make a very pretty sight.

The most crucial step in making any arrow is the fletching or placing of the feathers. While an arrow will fly without feathers, it will never be true. The three feathers, which constitute normal fletching, are spaced 120 degrees apart around the shaft, with the cock feather being perpendicular to the nock. When the arrow is ready to shoot, the cock feather sticks out

to the left of the bow and the other two, the hen feathers, rest equally on the bow as the arrow is released. In flight the feathers, or vanes, catch the air and keep the head of the arrow straight. The natural curve of the vanes is such that when they are placed on the shaft, along the axis, there is a certain amount of spiral, which serves to turn the arrow along the axis in its flight. Some archers prefer arrows which have even more spin than is provided by the natural curve of the vanes, so that when they do their fletching they set the arrows on at an angle to the axis, taking care that the angle remains constant for all three vanes. No one has, as yet, proved that either method is superior to the other and the best advice is to try both. You may or may not have a preference, but it is impossible to tell, without testing.

Turkey feathers are today's leading source of arrow vanes. The "grey goose feather" has, for some unknown reason, lost its great popularity, although there is no reason for you not to try it. Either kind of feather is easy to obtain. Many modern fletchers buy their feathers already cut, but since we are working on the assumption that you want to make as much of your equipment as possible, we'll assume that you want to make your own vanes.

First and foremost, remember that there is a left and a right to feathers. The natural curve is not the same on both wings and the surest way in the world to get a poor

Arrows and Arrow Making

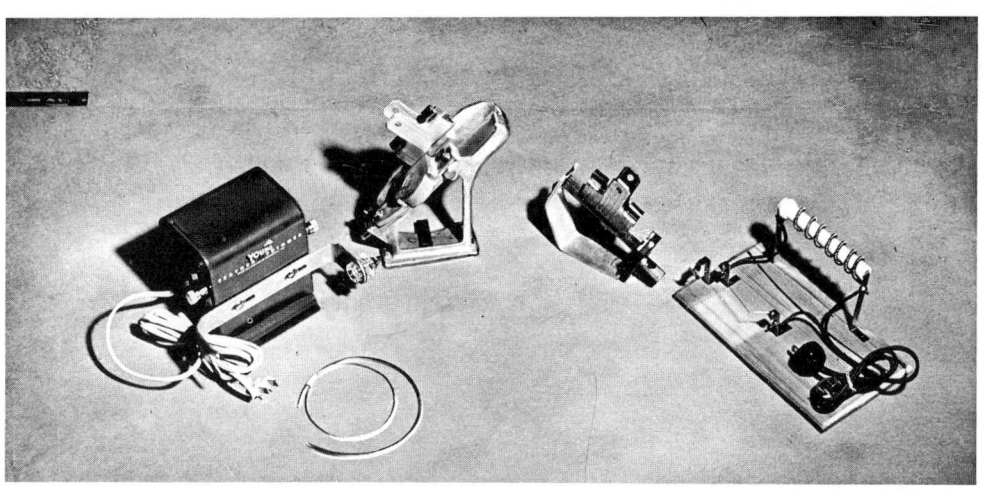

Feather-trimming instruments may be bought cheaply by amateurs: here are electric and clamp types.

An array of various kinds of arrows: at left are fishing, field and hunting types; at right, target.

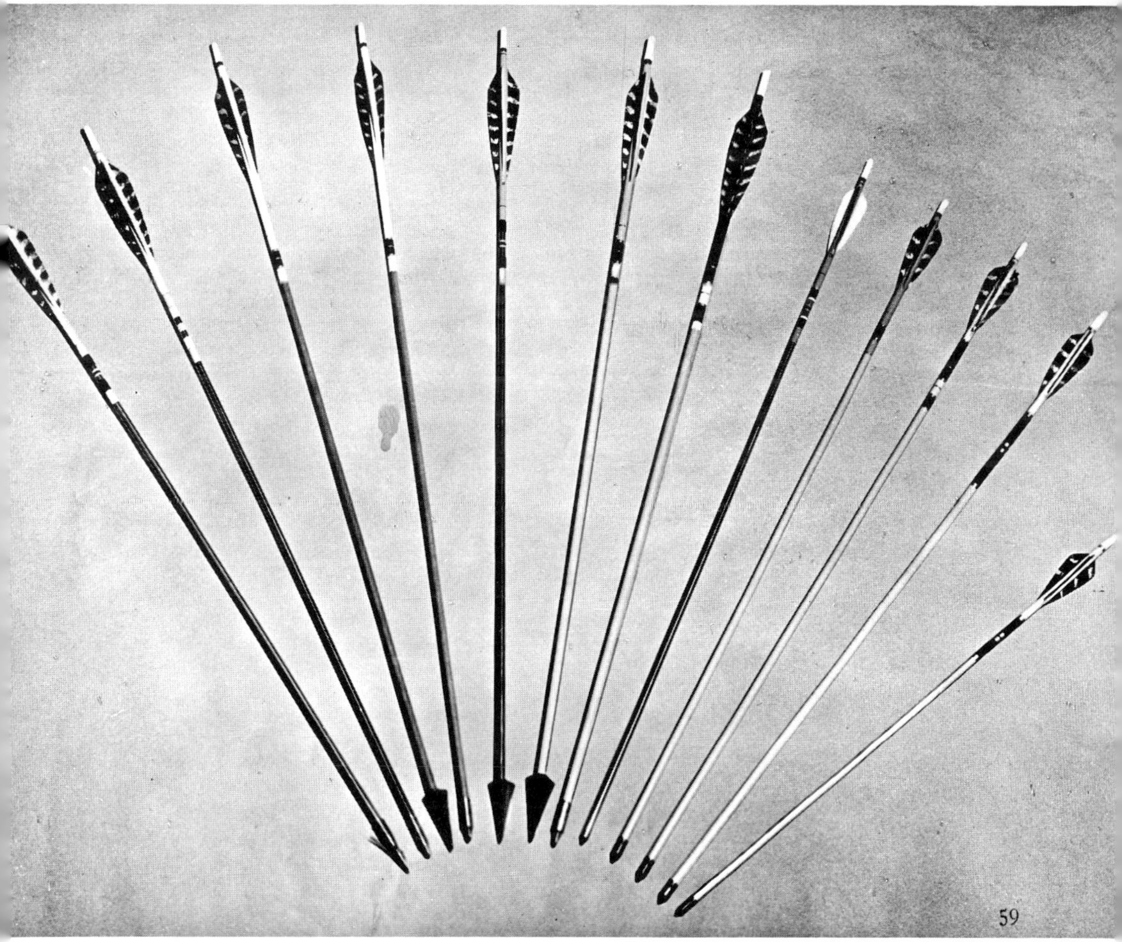

59

Photo by Grayson Tewksberry, Fawcett Studio
Flint heads, courtesy of their maker, Jim Ramsey

Flint and obsidian arrow heads are the best hunting points for big game but require special skill to make.

and often dangerous arrow, is to fletch it with feathers from both wings of a bird. **When you select your feathers, be sure that you work with all lefts or all rights.** The only feathers of interest to us are the pinions, the long strong ones that occur on the outside of the wings. The rest of the bird's plumage may be handsome, but for the fletcher's purpose, it's useless.

There are two ways of getting the vanes out of the feathers so that you can use them —stripping and paring. Again, there's disagreement among archers as to which method is the best. The first great author on archery, Roger Ascham, felt that stripping was a lazy, ineffective method. But on the other hand, most of the commercially produced arrows in this country are made with stripped vanes—and one cannot complain about the quality of their flight. To avoid taking sides in the quarrel, we'll describe both methods and let you take your pick.

In stripping, the trick comes with practice and it's a good plan to start with a few feathers that aren't top grade so you can afford to do a little experimentation. Take the feather in your left hand, holding the tip of the small end between your thumb and fingers, being sure that the quill will not slip. Bring your right hand in and grasp the vein of the feather, as close to your left thumb as possible. Then begin to pull, down. **Don't try to pull away from the feather, but always down it.** The vein or web will come away from the main body of the quill, much more easily than you might expect. You should have the feather quite clean, with only a thin strip of quill adhering to the base. When you've completed that much, cut the ends neatly, so that you'll have even ends to work with.

Paring is the more difficult way of getting your vanes, since it requires that you make minute, perfect cuts. A single-edge razor blade is your best tool for paring. Take the feather and split the quill from top to bottom with the blade, starting from the point, or thick end of the quill. You'll have to cut very carefully, since you want to work as closely as possible to the web. without cutting into it, or leaving an excess of quill along the base of your vane. If your cut is correct, you next put the web on a smooth surface and pare away any excess quill, especially the thick ridge running

ARROWS AND ARROW MAKING

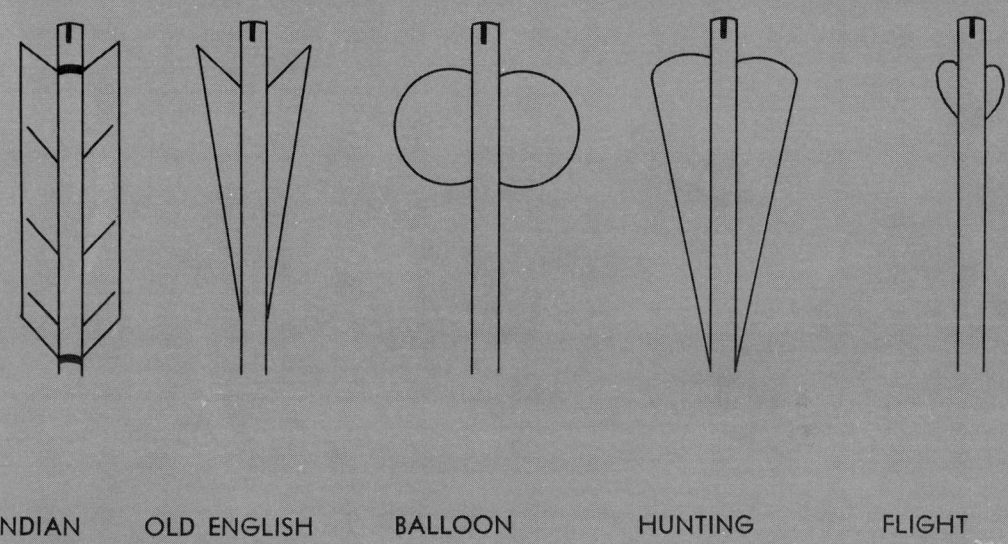

FEATHER CUTS USED IN FLETCHING

INDIAN   OLD ENGLISH   BALLOON   HUNTING   FLIGHT

Diagrams above show classic feather-shapes and may be used as a guide by amateur arrow makers.

along the back. To finish, put the web into a clamp paper clip, with the quill edge out and work it smooth on a very fine grade of sandpaper.

Having gotten the vanes, by stripping or cutting, our next problem is to position them on the shaft. Most commercial arrows have a cock feather of a contrasting color to the hen feathers, to give you a ready check when you're out shooting. You may or may not want to make this difference yourself. If you do, select a group of feathers (always from the same side) which are contrasty in color and reserve them for use as cock feathers. Another method and a simple one, is to dye a group of feathers, for use as cocks.

The feathers are placed, as we said before, at 120 degrees from each other along the axis of the shaft wood. While they should be placed as close to the nock as possible, you have to allow room for the fingers. Spacing then, from the nock, is normally anywhere from 1 in. to 1½ in. Select the distance you'll want and mark the shafts on which you're working, so that each one will be fletched the same. Vanes vary—both in their natural curve and in the angle at which the web stands on the quill base—so when you go to place the vanes in position, see to it that the vanes are at 120 degrees to each other, not merely to the bases on which they stand. Your cock feather, which is set 180 degrees from the nock is glued on first. Since there are two spots on the diameter which will accommodate the cock feather you have, at least in theory, a choice. But there is one thing you may take into consideration in making your choice. Examine the wood carefully and you'll see that the grain comes to the surface in a series of roughly concentric long triangles, in many instances. On the side of the wood which will run along the side of the bow the grain should be close and parallel. You must, for safety's sake see to it that the tips of the grain triangles run backward toward the nock—for the reason that if your arrow ever gives, it will do so along these lines and the chances of injury are much lessened by setting them up this way.

Having selected the one spot for your cock feather, you're ready for your actual gluing. There are many glues on the market but for arrow work you have to select one

CHART A

ARROW LENGTH	15-27 LBS.	28-35 LBS.	36-45 LBS.	46-60 LBS.	60 LBS.
16"	9/32"				
18"	9/32"				
22½"	9/32"				
24"	9/32"	9/32"	5/16"		
25"	9/32"	9/32"	5/16"	21/64"	21/64"
26"	9/32"	5/16"	5/16"	21/64"	11/32"
27"	9/32"	5/16"	5/16"	21/64"	11/32"
28"	5/16"	5/16"	21/64"	11/32"	11/32"
29"	5/16"	21/64"	11/32"	11/32"	11/32"
30"	5/16"	21/64"	11/32"	11/32"	11/32"
ARROW LENGTH	**BOW WEIGHT AT YOUR DRAWING LENGTH**				

which is not affected by moisture. The arrows are often dampened in shooting and it is no fun to lose feathers when you're in the field. The simplest glue to use is common household cement, which is easy to apply and dries rapidly. Casein glue is even better, but since it's slow drying, you have to pin or bind the vanes in place while the glue dries. Of course if you make an error, this slow drying has its advantages, because you can reset the vanes without harm.

For our purposes however, let's assume that household cement is your choice. Mark the cock feather's position with a pencil line and along that line spread a small amount of the cement. While that is getting tacky, smear the bottom of the vane with the cement and put it in place, working from the nock forward. Be very careful to avoid getting any glue on the actual vanes. If you slip and do, be sure to clean off the glue carefully. The veins of the feather must always slant backward. The cock feather is now fletched.

Your next job is to find the spots for the other feathers. Most fletchers set them by eye, but if you don't trust your sense of proportion, a small pair of dividers will enable you to get the positions exactly. Once you have the lines pencilled in you simply follow the same procedure used with the cock feather and the work is done. Stand the arrow to one side, in a rack or a deep glass, so that the arrangement of the vanes won't be spoiled as they might be by laying the arrow on its side.

If you use a slower drying glue, put the feathers in position and keep them there by wrapping with cotton thread. This will hold them to the shaft, while their relation to their axis can be controlled by putting straight pins into the wood, alongside the vanes.

Basically, your arrow is complete now. It can be shot, and unless you've made some serious error, it will fly fairly true. All that remains to do is to trim the vanes and crest the shaft. Trimming the vanes is governed by what you want to use the arrow for—vane shapes have varied, as long as man has shot the bow. There is probably no possible shape that hasn't been used.

The length of the vanes varies greatly. A target arrow will carry a set of vanes

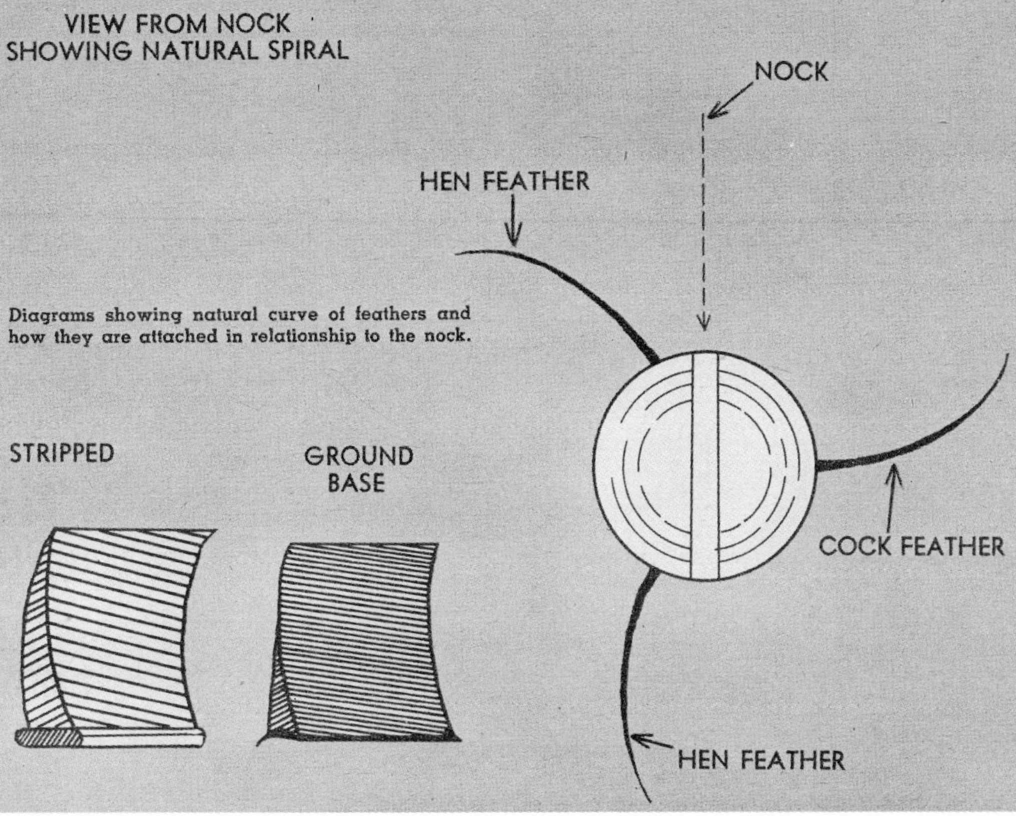

ARROWS AND ARROW MAKING

VIEW FROM NOCK SHOWING NATURAL SPIRAL

Diagrams showing natural curve of feathers and how they are attached in relationship to the nock.

STRIPPED **GROUND BASE**

NOCK **HEN FEATHER** **COCK FEATHER** **HEN FEATHER**

that are from two to three inches long, while a hunting arrow will have vanes as long as five inches. The difference is necessary because of the difference in the weight of the piles or heads. Since the purpose of the fletching is to keep that head pointed at the target, it would be silly to use too little surface with a big head and conversely too much surface with a small head is pointless.

The actual shape of the vane can, and often does remain the same for target arrows and hunting arrows. Thus, if you choose a modified balloon trim for your target shafts, it will probably be 2½ in. long and just short of a ½ in. through at its deepest point. With a hunting arrow the same form will be followed but the extreme measurements will be 5½ in. long with a depth of ¾ in. at the deep point.

To assure getting trims that are alike you can easily make a template in the pattern of your choice and use it when you trim. Or make a double template, which will enclose the vane area to be used, leaving you free to dispose of the rest, with a scissors or a razor blade. Be sure that when you cut, you work from the back forward. If you plan to fletch many arrows, you'll have to find another, faster method, such as a die, which uses old razor blades for its cutting edge. A fairly new tool for trimming, is an electrically heated wire which is bent to conform to your selected pattern and then run across the vane.

With the fletching completed you have only to crest your arrows and the job is finished. Cresting serves to make the arrows look better and, more important, it lets you tell your arrows from those of the next archer. The pattern you choose may be simple or complicated, according to your own tastes. Use a waterproof paint and for the extra touch that makes for a professional job, put a fine, fine line of black between the larger color areas.

It's a good plan to number your arrows. When you're practicing you know that, say Arrow No. 6 flirts a little and that Arrow No. 9 has a tendency to fly a little to the right. Before you can establish the flight characteristics of the different shafts, you'll have to practice with them, of course. But it's simpler if you number each one. Use tiny decal numbers or paint the numbers on when you're doing the cresting.

Variety of available equipment matches the wide range of archery enthusiasts, from young to old.

EQUIPMENT COST AND BOW BREAKDOWN

Equipment Cost
and
Bow Breakdown

Archery equipment can be as expensive in cost or as reasonable as you wish: complete practice set can be made for under $15.00.

THE cost of archery equipment is more than reasonable. With a few basic tools at hand, you can make all your equipment—bow, string, arrows, quiver, tab—for less than fifteen dollars. This figure is based on good grade material, but does not include the finest available. For not much more money, even the finest can be had.

The biggest single item in the budget will be your bow stave. And yet, while it is the biggest in one sense, it may not be from a dollar standpoint. The average lemonwood stave, suitable for either a flat bow or a long bow, will cost you from two to three dollars. The comparable stave in hickory runs about a dollar cheaper. In yew or osage, it is easier to buy billets, which must be joined with a fish-tail joint in order to make the bow. These two top bow woods run from ten to twelve dollars a pair for billets. Some dealers offer the billets already fishtailed and glued at a nominal extra cost.

The string material will cost you nearly as much as your stave, but you'll have to remember that this cost, while high originally, will yield you many strings from the one ball of material. Flax is the least expensive, running slightly over a dollar for a ball of two ounces. The synthetics—fortisan and dacron—are nearly three dollars for a four-ounce spool. Wax which you can get from your shoemaker, or buy mixed with resin from a tackle dealer, costs only a few cents.

Arrows, you'll find, are actually your most expensive item. Again, bear in mind that a cheap arrow, or rather a poor one, is a bad investment. You certainly won't want the best arrows in the world, when you first start to practice, but you will want the best you can make. Feathers, which are sometimes in short supply, will cost between seventy-five cents and a dollar a hundred, already cut, ground and dyed. Nocks, of the plastic variety, run about fifty cents a dozen and piles are variously priced, depending on the grade and type you

Photo showing young
N. Y. State champion archer,
Bruce Baker, is by Kelly Studio,
courtesy Stuart Wilson, Jr., president
of N. Y. State Field Archery Association

Photo below, courtesy Paul Bunyan Bait Co.; at right, photo by Fawcett Studio

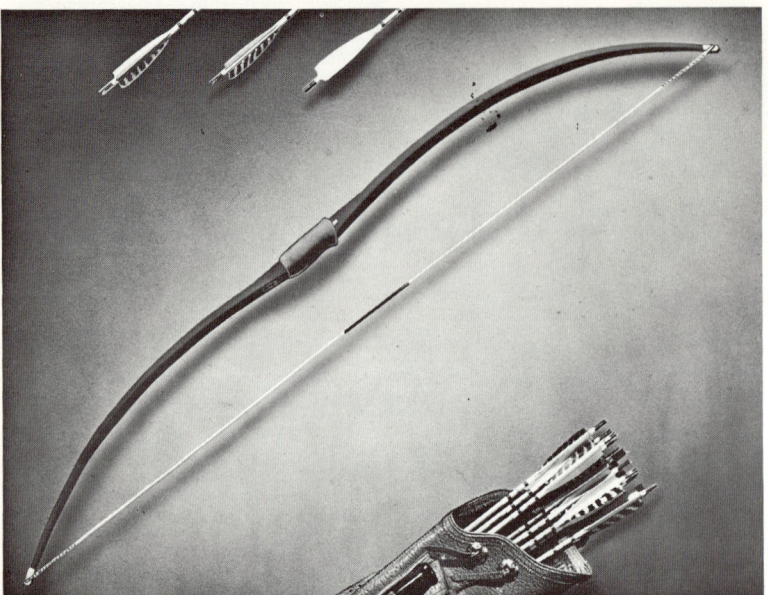

Standard reflex bow shown here is made of Fiberglas, low in cost and very popular among beginning archers. Bow at right is laminated wood and plastic.

want. A good set of a dozen practice piles, suitable for field work costs approximately one dollar. The shafts themselves can be as cheap or as costly as you wish. Port Orford Cedar dowels, unmatched (you can match them for grade and spine yourself), cost less than ten cents apiece in quantity lots. At the other end of the price range are the lovely aluminum shafts, matched and tested. These bits of metal cost around a dollar and seventy-five cents per shaft, and are to be shot with care.

Leather, wool, scraps of material are all available locally and to attempt to estimate local prices is pointless. But again, with a few tools and the basic items, you can make your own tackle, inexpensively.

On the other hand, you may want to buy your equipment ready-made. In which case you may want an approximation of its total cost. While still not an expensive sport, archery is a lot more costly if you go out to the store for everything you need:

We'll discuss the cost of bows next. First, let's look at the over-all picture of American bowyers. There are several large manufacturers of archery equipment in the country who specialize in bow-making. Their products are almost universally well made, shoot well, and are ideal for beginners or for school and club work.

Then there are the custom bowyers, whose products are prized by archers, as some people prize antiques or fine china. In an age when mass production is the watchword, it is a distinct pleasure to find men who still work as skilled artisans, turning out few finished products, but each of them a masterpiece.

In the middle ground of production are a few firms, whose output is larger than the custom craftsman, but who still do not come under the mass production heading. They are almost without exception men who were formerly custom makers and who, through the press of demand, enlarged their facilities to accommodate their customers.

It is a pleasure to say that if you go out to buy a bow—or any piece of archery equipment—you are dealing with reputable people, whose business word is their bond. Perhaps a large part of that is due to the fact that almost without exception the makers are archers themselves.

On the opposite page is an analysis of the various bows in the four categories. •

```
Quivers:
    Hunting  ........ $4.00 to $20.00
    Target   ..........  1.00 to   4.00
    Ground   ..........  2.00 to   4.00
Arm Guards ..........  1.00 to   3.00
Tabs, etc  ..........   .75 to   2.50
Strings    ..........  1.00 to   2.00
Arrows     ..........  6.00 to  30.00
                        (Per dozen)
```

EQUIPMENT COST AND BOW BREAKDOWN

BOW BREAKDOWN

	BOW	STYLE	LENGTH	PULL IN POUNDS	MAKER	COMMENT
MASS PRODUCED	Kodiak	Recurve	62"-66"	To 100	Bear Archery Co.	The Bear line of bows is widely known and highly respected. All the bows are made with maple cores and fiberglas backs and bellies. Each bow is registered and guaranteed by maker.
	Cub	Flat	62"	To 60	Same	
	Eddings Super-Cast	Reflexed	62"	To 75	Eddings Archery	A reflexed and semi-working recurve bow with toxhorn facing and fiberglas backing.
	Stallion	Recurve	60"	50 to 60	Centaur Archery Co.	An excellently made bow of perfect balance. Manufacturer registers and guarantees each bow for a year and will replace or repair his product if it fails to work properly. Has a maple core, fiberglas backing and toxhorn facing.
CUSTOM	Na-Po	Recurve	Varies	Varies	Hugh Rich	Excellent workmanship. Uses same type lamination as Bear Bows.
	Folberth	Turkish Recurve	62"-74"	To 70	Folberth Arrows	One of the greatest of the custom bows. Holds 8 national and world records. Many modern bows use one or all three of Folberth's patents.
	Professional	Working Recurve	62"-69"	To 65	Hoyt Archery	Another top custom bow with several records. Incorporates one of the Folberth patents. Made of fiberglas, wood and plastic.
	Drake Composite	Recurve	Varies	Varies	Drake Archery	Drake bows hold most of the world flight records. Hard to acquire they are the flight-shooter's pet. Now makes field and target bows as well.
	Eicholtz	Working Recurve	Varies	Varies	Frank Eicholtz	Wood cores with plastic facings and backings. Excellent bows.
GLASS	Paul Bunyan	Working Recurve	61"	To 60	Paul Bunyan Glass Products	A solid glass bow, very sweet in shooting. Cannot shatter or snap. Unaffected by temperature and can be left braced. Unconditionally guaranteed for one year.
	Stream-Eze	Working Recurve	54"	To 65	Archery Sales & Service	A good glass bow, made for ready take-down.
	Royal Huntsman	Working Recurve	Varies	Varies	Veneko Tackle Co.	Fiberglas with laminated wood handle. Fourteen-month guarantee. Highly recommended by top flight archers.
	Turk	Turkish Recurve	4'6"	To 60	E. Bud Pierson	A top grade glass bow, backed by the Pierson reputation. Incorporates Folberth design.
METAL	Jet	Reflex	61"	To 60	American Archery	A good, inexpensive metal bow of aluminum. Flat trajectory but jars the hand somewhat.
	Hunter	Recurve	54"	To 64	Grimes Archery	First of the aluminum bows. Demountable with replacement limbs. Good cast, smooth action.
	Kestral	Reflex	60"	To 42	Apollo	English bow of tubular steel. Has flat trajectory and is smooth although too light for most hunting.
	Tiger	Reflex	Varies	To 64	Seefab	Called the aristocrat of metal bows. Tiger is imported from Sweden, made of charcoal steel. Built as a take-down model, it is guaranteed for 200,000 shots.

For less expensive equipment the archer has a dozen choices. Perhaps the largest maker of tackle in the cheaper grades is Ben Pearson of Pine Bluff, Ark. Another big maker is the Robin Hood Co., of Montclair, New Jersey. Also the Centaur Archery Co., Glenshaw, Pennsylvania, makes a cheaper bow called the "Mustang."

How to Use Equipment

Photo by Pinney from Monkmeyer

how TO USE EQUIPMENT

A mastery of form is of prime importance to an archer, but it's not as difficult as it may seem if each step is learned separately as detailed in the following pages.

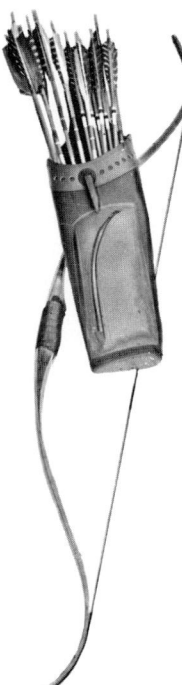

GOOD shooting with a bow and arrow is a matter of practice—like any other sport which depends on the individual and his coordination. It is no more reasonable to expect a total novice to pick up a racket and walk off with the local tennis championship, than it is to expect to take your new bow and put six arrows in the gold at eighty yards or drop a running buck at forty.

But once you have mastered form, there are years and years of sport ahead of you, in field, tournament or hunting. So, it's a matter of getting the basics firmly fixed in your mind. Emphasis on form may seem strange in archery, but again, as in other sports it is a matter of necessity, if you want to be successful. Remember, an archer with bad style may occasionally shoot a good score—but he won't do it consistently. And consistency of style is the only way to hit your mark repeatedly.

The first thing to learn is how to string or brace your bow properly. There is in existence somewhere a detailed list which tells you how to string a bow while standing in midstream, how to string it while riding at full gallop on horseback and how to string it while lying flat on your back. Since none of us is likely to be called on to perform any of these feats, we'll confine our stringing instructions to those for the straight bow (long or flat) and the recurved. With the straight bow (all these remarks are addressed to right-handers; if you're left handed, reverse them) take the handle in your left hand, with the back of the bow facing you. Put the lower end of the bow against the inside of the arch of your left foot, keeping the tip off the ground. With the right hand, guide the loop up toward the nock of the upper limb. *Keep your fingers out of the loop*—a slip here might cost you

One of the 5 basic steps of good form is this: drawing the arrow must be done with steady ease.

The stance is another basic step: the archer stands at right angles to target with feet firm.

69

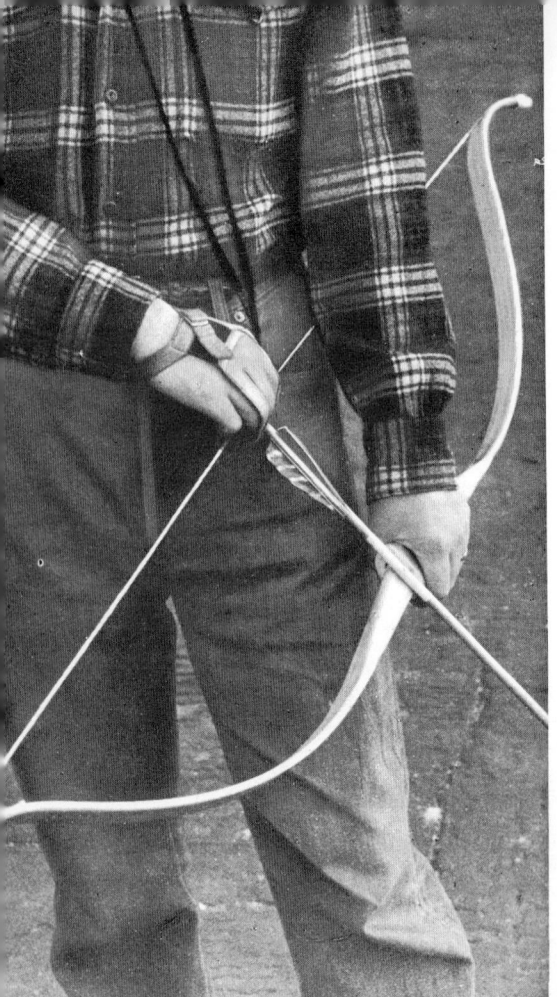

a fingernail, if the bow is heavy. At the same time you're slipping the loop up, the left hand is pulling and the two forces—push with the right and pull with the left—will enable you to slip the loop over the nock and into place. To unbrace the bow, follow the same procedure, except that when enough force is exerted to slip the loop free, bring it back down on the upper limb, not out and off the end.

The recurve bow is a little harder to brace because of its construction. (If your straight bow is too heavy to string by the method given above, apply the recurve bracing style.) But once the trick is mastered it is very simple. Put the lower limb across your left ankle, so that the curve goes back, then step through the string. The bow will now have its handle behind your right thigh and the curve of the lower limb across your left ankle. Bring your left hand across the front of your body and guide the loop into the upper nock, while your right arm is bringing the upper limb forward from the rear. Again, reverse the steps to unbrace the bow.

Let's look at actual shooting. Many, many years ago, Roger Ascham, who was the tutor of Queen Elizabeth I, wrote the first book in English on archery, which today is still the real bible of the archer.

Shown on this page are common errors made by beginners when nocking an arrow.

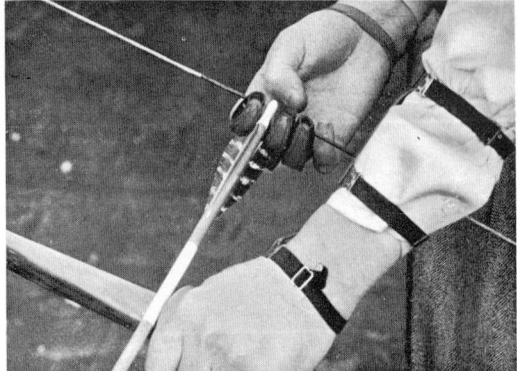

Above, arrow is being gripped between fingers and cannot slide easily into nock.

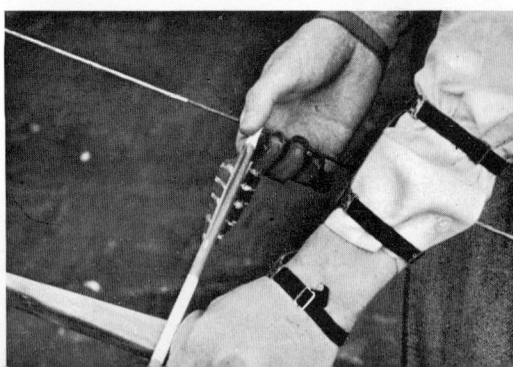

At center, arrow is almost correct, but thumb is wrong; below, never thumbgrab.

how TO USE EQUIPMENT

Ascham divided shooting into five parts and the best archers who've come after him haven't been able to make a better division. Ascham said, in part:

"Standinge, nockinge, drawing, holdinge, lowsing, whereby cometh fayre shootinge, which neyther belong to winde nor wether, nor yet to the marke, for in a raine and at no marke, a man may shoote a fayre shote."

Standing then is the first thing we have to consider, and there have been books written on standing, alone. Our concern is not with the handsomest stance, but with the one which will yield you the best shots. Your feet should be roughly parallel, at ninety degrees to your target. On the range you can put marks in the ground, where your toes hit and be sure that you regain the same spot every time, but in the field it's impossible. Also, in the field and hunting, you're often in a spot where it's physically impossible to get your feet parallel, or on the same level—in fact you may shoot kneeling, sitting or lying down.

In general, stand with your feet at right angles to the target, with the left side of your body in profile to it. How far apart your feet should be is a matter of the person involved. John may keep his feet well together and Pete, next to him, stand with a two foot gap between his legs. Both men may score equally well—but Pete has the edge. A wide stance gives you a good brace and somehow has the quality of giving you assurance. Don't try to keep your knees locked and the muscles of the legs tensed. That'll work for the first thirty arrows but after that, the muscles begin to tire and rebel and a muscle cramp is no more fun in archery than it is in a swimming pool.

Perhaps you've wondered why, in listing the points to be observed, Ascham did not mention aiming, specifically? The answer to that question is that all five divisions are part of aiming. The archer is actually aiming as he takes his stand, even though he himself may not be aware of it. From the moment the archer picks up his bow until the arrow is well flown, he is aiming.

Going back to the stance for a moment, try a number of variants—then pick the one that suits you best. Ascham's advice was to be comfortable, to choose the position best suited *to you*. Ascham's still right. Only remember that full draw exerts a lot of different pressures on various parts of your body—you'll need firm balance. And the second point to bear in mind is that once you've chosen a stance—stick with it. Excellence in archery lies in repeating that which is good and eliminating

Correct way to nock arrow: hold between forefinger, middle finger; bring arrow back flush with string.

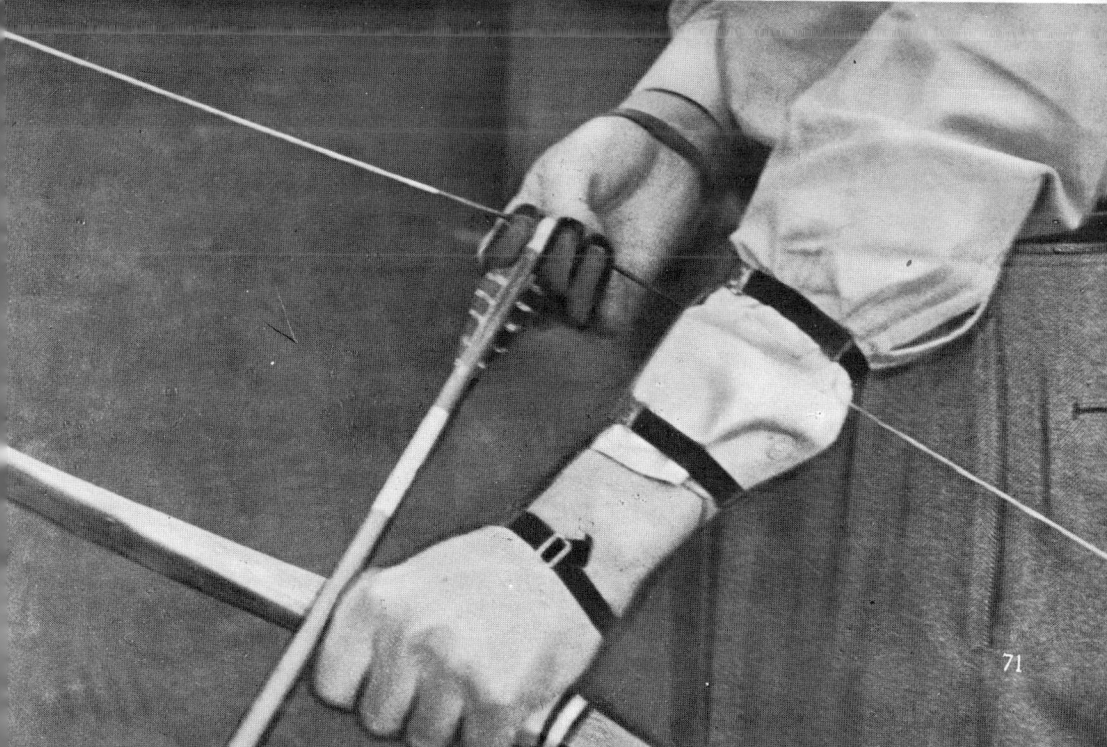

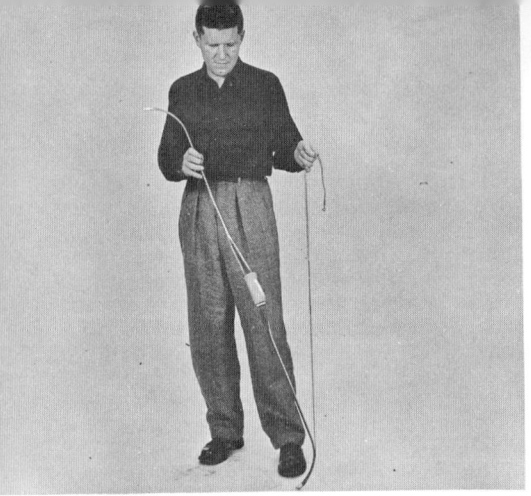

First step in stringing a recurve bow: place string in bow-nock at lower end, snug in curve-groove.

Now support lower bow-curve with left leg as shown and step over top of bow with right leg.

All photos on these two pages by the Fawcett Studio

the things which vary from shot to shot.

Nocking is the easiest of Ascham's precepts, since it deals only with placing the arrow on the string. The nock of the arrow is held between the forefinger and middle finger of the string hand and the arrow lies flat along the upper side of the bow. Bring the nock back until it is flush with the string, and you have nocked it. There are two things only to bear in mind—one, the cock feather must be away from the side of the bow, and two, the arrow must be nocked at the same point on the string for every shot. To insure your placing the arrow correctly, fix your nocking point and mark the position with ink. Then, just above and below that point on the string, wind a few turns of dental floss or silk thread. It becomes instinctive for you to get the arrow in that immediate area, but with the aid of the double serving, you'll have no need to even look at the string. To test the need for this try an experiment. Nock an arrow so the shaft lies along the arrow plate, but with the nock a quarter-inch below the usual point. Shoot the arrow and mark its flight, then do the same thing with a second arrow, only this time, nock it above the normal point. The big difference in the flight of the two shafts will more than persuade you of the necessity for a nocking point marked on your string.

With the arrow on the string, you're ready to draw. The bow, held in the left hand is parallel to the ground, gripped at the handle by the left hand, with the upper limb of the bow pointing to the right. The three first fingers of the palm-up right hand are on the string, above and below the arrow. The forefinger is above, the other two below. There will be no need for them to hold the nock—it should fit the string so that a slight tap is necessary for it to drop free.

The next step, like everything else in archery, has dozens of variations and hundreds of adherents for every variation. And again, *choose the method best suited to you and stick with it,* remembering that freedom from tension is the greatest asset you can have when you shoot.

The bow is brought from the horizontal to the vertical and as it is, the left arm pushes forward and the right arm draws back. Lengthy articles have been written about the amount of effort each arm must

Bring top curve of bow forward bracing handle on right thigh, place string in groove, noose in nock.

HOW TO USE EQUIPMENT

exert—some people have even gone so far as to recommend that the left arm go forward to the position of full draw and let the right do all the work. Such a practice may be good for the rare individual, but for most of us the arms go up and the arrow comes sliding back until the pile is resting on the arrow shelf, without any thought as to which arm is doing the lion's share of the work.

When you reach that point, stop for a few seconds and do some checking. Incidentally, you should be able to hold for that length of time, unless you are overbowed. The weight of the string should be on the *tips* of the three drawing fingers. Don't let the string ride over toward the inside of the fingers into the crease that forms the knuckle or else your release will be poor. The fingers must be at right angles to the string and they should be close together. The wrist and forearm should form a continuation of the arrow, with the elbow high. If the elbow is high, the shoulder muscles are doing the work and that is the correct method. The bow should be held firmly, but not tightly—with the weight of the bow held hard to the soft pad of flesh under the thumb. Actually, many target archers hold the bow so loosely that on the release the bow jumps free from the hand and slides to the ground. It is definitely incorrect to hold the bow in a rigid, death-defying grip. *The bow should be held firmly but not tightly.* The elbow of the left arm should be straight as is the wrist.

There is another point which should be brought up here. In the old records of archery we find mention made of "laying the body in the bow." Certainly the records show that the English archers used this method with their great long bows. It is an instinctive act and one which you may find yourself doing without any direct thought.

With a light bow, the draw places no strain on the archer, but as you begin to work with heavier bows it is sometimes difficult to achieve full draw. It's with the big bows then that you lay the body in. Halfway through the draw, with the left arm coming up to the vertical and the right arm going back you really begin to feel the full weight of the bow. As we have tried to emphasize, this whole action must

To string a flat bow: place lower nock against shoe-edge as shown, never on the floor or ground.

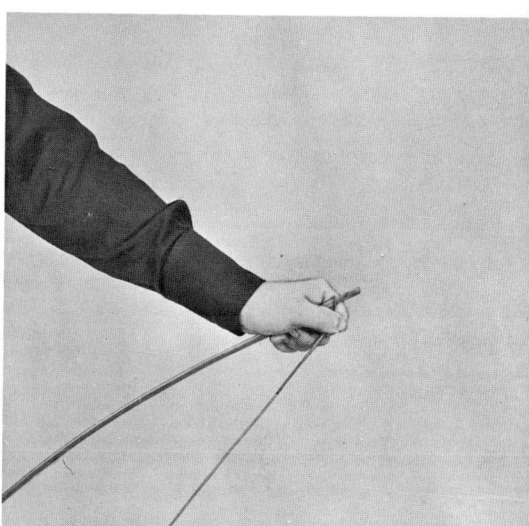

Slide string into nock and flat bow is strung. Study photo below for position of hands and grip.

With one end of bow supported on shoe, bend other end forward as you bring string up to nock.

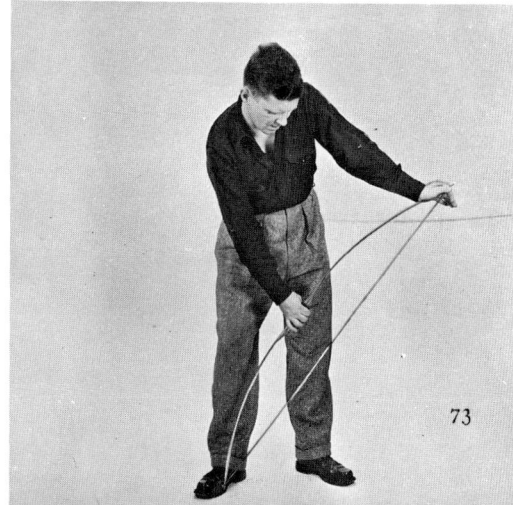

Aiming is done several ways: archer here is using "kisser," small button positioned on string.

Button can be seen, below, after release: it is held between teeth at full draw for uniform draws.

be a natural one. You can't shoot successfully if your actions are strained or artificial. At this instant if the bow feels too tough, square your shoulders and stick out your chest, just exactly as if you were trying to get it into the space between the string and the bow. You'll find that the rest of the draw will come easily and without effort. Whether or not there is a real movement in toward the bow, it's hard to say—but whether the move is psychological or physical, it will serve the purpose.

The bow is drawn now and you are at what is called the anchor. And here is where you will have to make a definite choice, unless you want to use two anchors.

The anchor point is the spot on your face or head where the string presses when the arrow is at full draw. Just as the arrow must always be drawn to the full—and no more—for every shot, so the anchor point must remain constant. Without full draw and without the same anchor point you can never hope to drive two arrows into the same spot with anything but pure luck.

Most modern anchor points are to the lips, with the fingers held just under the chin. This way the string forms a line that bisects the face. In order to keep this point from moving, small buttons are fastened on the string, or layers of thin tape wrapped round. The resulting "kisser" is moved up and down the string until the archer finds the correct anchor point with the kisser between his teeth. He has succeeded in putting the arrow in full draw at a certain spot, eliminating one more possible variant.

The hunting archer, on the other hand, usually chooses an anchor point farther back on his face. For this reason the field or hunting archer tilts both his head and his bow, since with the high anchor the string comes well to the right of his eye. The tilt compensates for this, bringing the eye over the arrow again.

For a matter of seconds—probably four at the most—hold the position. Mentally run over the checklist of what you should be doing and correct any slight (we hope slight) errors you may be making. Then release.

With the three-finger or Mediterranean release, the fingers slip back off the string without any creep forward. In fact, creep is one of the archer's worst enemies. The string must slip smoothly from the fingers, or the arrow will fly to one side or the other. As the tension is released by the fingers, both the right arm, which is straining back, and the left, which is pushing for-

HOW TO USE EQUIPMENT

ward, will continue a slight motion in their respective lines of force. But only the finger muscles are allowed to relax. The position should be held until the arrow is well on its way. Many people wait until the arrow has struck before they drop their arms.

The loose, which looks simple, is the hardest part about shooting. You must not pluck the string backward and you must not let the fingers creep forward. They must simply let the string go. And remember that while there is a very slight movement of the bow arm—it must be just that. When the bow is at full draw the left arm stops working except as a carrier for the bow. Its work is done and any movement it injects at this point will only ruin the shot.

Basically then, that is all there is to shooting—stance, nock, draw, hold and loose. You may perfect the first four, but if you ever manage to get the perfect loose you'll have done something no archer in history has accomplished before.

We mentioned aiming shortly after the matter of getting the proper stance. To go more carefully into the matter, there are two styles of aiming—the instinctive and what is called "free-style." From a matter of personal preference the author is an instinctive shooter, but good though it may be, this style will never turn in the scores on the target rounds that the free-style archers get.

Instinctive shooting is a self-explanatory term. You are shooting at a target, alive or not, and you loose at that moment when your whole body tells you it is correct. There is little to be said to amplify such a definition. Let's examine an example of the coordination of mind and body which we all possess. Form your right hand into the pistol shape you used to make in the early "cowboy and Indian" days and then pick a target, either near or far. Without stopping to think, point your gun hand at that target. You'll find, that barring some physical deficiency, you're on target every time. When you're at full draw the bow hand has brought the bow to the right height, the other arm has drawn the arrow full. Your eye registers the bow and the arrow—*but out of focus.* Don't attempt to get them in focus. *Fix your attention on the target and the target only.* The spot on which you concentrate is the important thing; your mind is taking all the other data into consideration and acts accordingly. At that moment you've become a computer—feeding information through your eyes. If the wrong sight is set, the mind controlling the multiple muscular ac-

Bow is never clutched tightly, is always held loosely but firmly between top fingers, as shown.

Another way to assure uniformity of each draw: bring string back till it cuts across nose and lips.

On these two pages is a sequence showing form of tournament archer: here he is nocking his arrow.

He begins his draw with bow high and gradually brings it down, sighting and drawing at same time.

Nearing full draw, string is about to cut over his nose, lips: when it does he knows draw is right.

tions can't help giving a bad result. *But don't think about it.* The entire chain of action and reaction is automatic and subconscious. Volition can destroy accuracy as easily as incorrect data.

Now instinctive shooting is based on this same principle. That is not to say that if you choose the style as yours in archery that you'll hit your target with unerring accuracy—but that is because there are a number of other things which must be taken into consideration.

When the arrow leaves the bow it does not fly flat, but inscribes a long parabola to the earth's surface. The modern rifle shoots very flat and the gunner has little to worry about on ranges up to one hundred yards. The archer, however, with his much higher trajectory, must be equipped to calculate the rise and fall of his shaft, so that it intercepts the target without digging grass yards short or sailing leisurely over the top. If this sounds difficult, don't be discouraged—just try it. Pick out a target in an open safe area and try to hit it, without thought of yardage. You'll be amazed at how close you'll come, *instinctively.*

The great benefit in instinctive shooting derives from the fact that you are prepared to shoot at any distance, over unfamiliar terrain and varying circumstances. And that is a vital part of hunting or roving, as we'll see.

The free-style archers are the men who run up the fantastic scores in tournaments. Walk along the line at any major competition and you see every archer using either a sight or a point-of-aim. There are constant arguments as to the respective merits.

Given a bow, an arrow and a target, there is only one place from which the shooter,

how to USE EQUIPMENT

using proper form, can shoot point blank at the target and hit. If you are farther back from your target and aim dead at the center the arrow will drop short and if you're closer, the arrow will sail high.

Since the shooting line is fixed and the archer must release while standing on it, the only way to compensate for this fact is to choose an auxiliary target, or one at which you can aim point blank for the distance you're shooting. In other words, you aim at a spot, either closer to you or farther than the real target, which will yield a hit on the real target. Suppose, for example, that you are shooting at close range. If you aim directly at the bull of the target your arrow will go too high (because of its parabolic flight) so you pick a spot on the ground which is between you and the real target. Aiming point blank at this spot you loose your arrow and watch its flight. If it intercepts the target, then you have picked the proper point-of-aim for the distance. If it is too high or too low, you choose another spot on the ground which will adjust the flight of the arrow until it is proper. If your choice is correct and your form unvaried, you will then automatically score. At long ranges, where the arrow is on the down grade of the parabola, you have to pick a point-of-aim which is behind the real mark. Again, this must be changed until you have the proper range. Many archers use a twig, a leaf, or a bush for their point, but others, shooting on a fixed target, place a marker on the spot, which can be moved back and forth as the need arises. This is impossible to do when hunting, so that there, the point-of-aim must depend on past experience. An archer must be able to judge the distance and know his equipment well enough so that he instinctively chooses the proper stump to aim for if he wants to hit the big buck standing ten yards beyond. The great cry of the hunter is that this is a mechanical means of aiming and places too much reliance on artificiality. On the other hand a really topnotch point-of-aim archer will yield to few in the field since his eye is so trained at gauging distance that he removes the mechanical aspect of his shooting. To me, such an archer is shooting instinctively, and there seems to be such a

From left to right: string has reached "anchor point," or point where it presses on nose, lips; arrow is ready and archer releases it by opening fingers; bow is held loosely and spins in grip, but he holds his stance.

Below are diagrams of three different ways to establish a "point of aim," needed because of arrow flight.

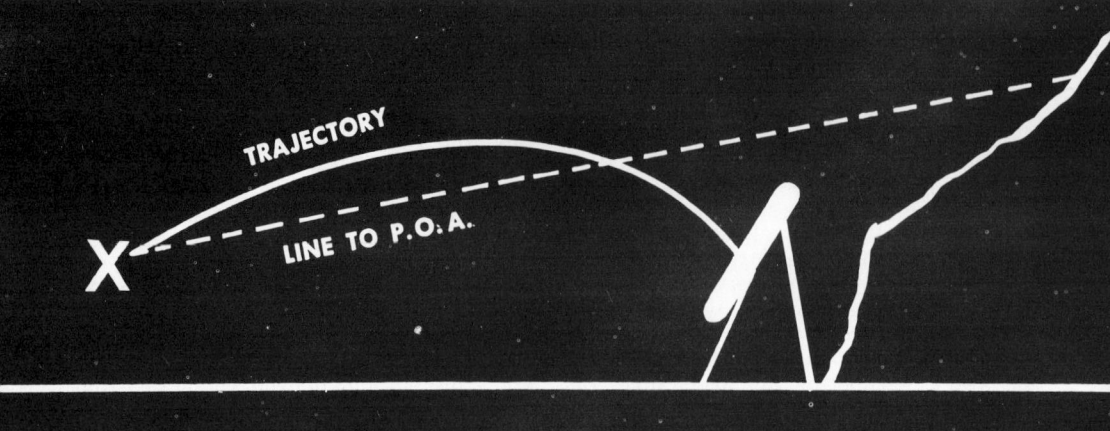

When target is far from archer, pick a point higher than bull's-eye and beyond, or arrow will fall short.

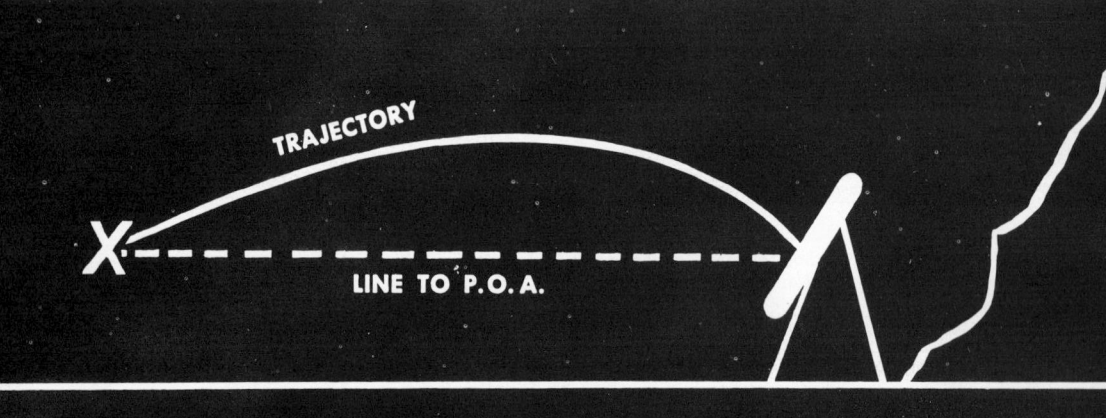

Dotted lines indicate goal, curved line indicates actual flight of arrow: above is medium-distance aim.

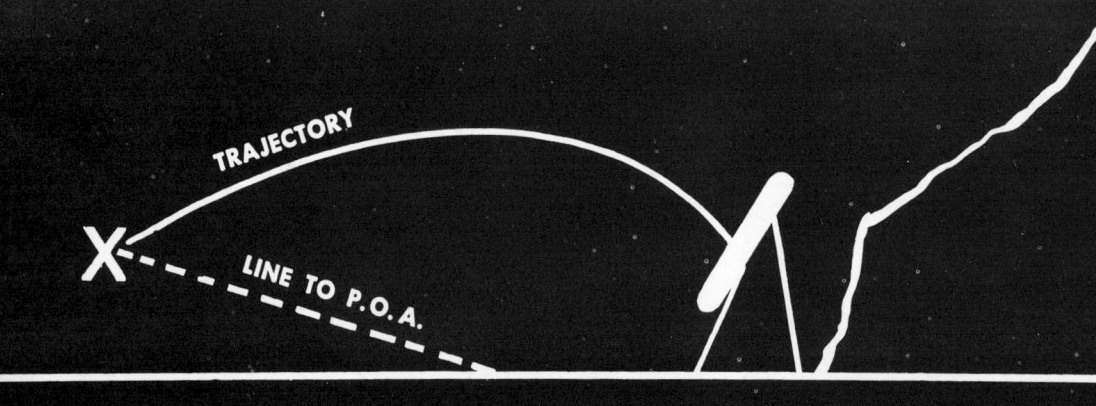

When standing close to target a spot must be picked out on ground for aim, or arrow will fly above gold.

How to Use Equipment

very fine line to draw between the two styles that it's hard to say which is which. Many an instinctive archer, who is concentrating solely on the target, has made the same calculations and absorbed the data into his problem without ever realizing it.

Bow sights, the last of the aiming classes, are comparatively new. They can be quite complicated—some of them are equipped with interchangeable prisms—or they may be extremely simple. The first bow sight the author ever saw was made from a wooden match and a rubber band. The match was fixed to the back of the bow with the band, so that it projected horizontally when the bow was drawn and since the band was movable, the match could be adjusted, up and down the back of the bow.

Essentially, that is all a sight is—a cross piece, fixed by some mechanical means, above the hand on the bow back. In effect, it puts the point-of-aim directly on the bow. From the simple rubber band-match sight, the next step is only logical. The archer marks the point on his bow where the match held when the range was forty yards, sixty yards and so on. The next time he comes to shoot at any of those distances he simply replaces the match or pin, or what have you to that spot and he is "sighted in."

The crucial thing about archery is practice; all the form and style in the world can't substitute for practice and more practice. If you'll apply what you've already learned to actual shooting—and keep at it —you'll turn in a first rate performance, on target or on game.

Most cities have archery ranges in their public parks, or if not, local clubs have ranges where members can practice. More and more you'll notice archery ranges replacing the old driving ranges throughout the country, so that you should have little trouble in finding a place to work out.

However, should you have difficulty in finding a practice area, it's simple to make your own. Check with the property owner before you begin. It's not only courteous, but it may save you a lot of trouble—landowners are nice people, but they resent, and rightfully so, invasion of their property.

Select, if you can, a field that is free from stones, running at least one hundred and fifty yards long and with any breadth over ten yards. Mark a line for shooting and measure a set of stakes from it—forty, sixty and eighty yards, with the last set at one hundred. Place your target on one of the stake lines and start shooting.

Standard targets, which are rather expensive and cumbersome, can be used, but it is possible to find a good substitute. A large cardboard carton, stuffed with corrugated cardboard is excellent, especially if you can fill the space between two of the pieces of corrugated board with sawdust. The box should be big enough so that you can mark a series of circles on one side, the largest of which will measure four feet across. The bull itself is 9.6 inches in diameter, and the other circles, which are concentric, are 4.8 inches wide. If you want your homemade target to conform to tournament rules, it should be set so it is four feet above the ground. The bull's-eye (gold) counts 9, the next ring (red) is 7, the next (blue) 5, the next (black) 3, and outer ring (white) is worth one. If you plan a fairly permanent setup, you can draw your faces on butcher's wrapping paper, and if you're so inclined, give them the standard colors—which adds to the picturesqueness of the shooting.

Having made your target, try all the distances you've marked, until you develop proficiency at any range. Take time to evaluate every shot you make—the time spent will amply repay you at a later date. If the arrows are flying low, find out why and change to correct the error. Make any changes that are necessary and then practice to develop consistency. There is no substitute for practice.

If you feel that you're going to be more interested in field archery and hunting, your practice will take another form. You shouldn't neglect the target range altogether, but your whole viewpoint on the subject of archery will be different. Field archery has but one purpose—to train the participants for actual hunting. For that reason, most of today's new converts are field archers. The appeal of hunting with a bow is strong and somehow strangely atavistic. Give a child a bow and he'll point it at the nearest bird, not the nearest bull's-eye.

Since you're bound to go hunting, your best plan is to simulate the conditions under which you'll find yourself later. Find some vacant land—the bigger an area the better—and again, ask permission to use it as a practice range. With this moving type of shooting, you'll have to be especially careful about livestock. Having gotten your permission, and we'll assume that it won't be too hard to do so, go out and select a natural target. Shoot for it and when you

Series of photos on these two pages shows real champ form by Ann Weber Corby, U. S. champ.

Note Ann's stance as she prepares to draw on the target line: feet firmly planted, arrow nocked.

Ann draws gracefully to her "anchor point." Note that her stance has not changed the slightest.

Side view of champion stance: study height and straightness of Ann's drawing arm, position of feet.

How to Use Equipment

Arrow has been loosed toward target: champ form demands release-position be held until it strikes.

Close-up view, above, of one kind of "anchor point," using nose, chin and lips to determine right draw.

This little girl is learning form but still has few lessons to go: bow-grip too tight, stance loose.

how to USE EQUIPMENT

recover your arrows, pick another and so work yourself around the area. This is the simplest form of what is called "roving" but it's also the best solo practice for the field shooter. And take care to use sturdy arrows—shooting around the hills and pastures will cause a lot of shaft casualties. A hidden rock is no respecter of good wood, but these natural hazards are things you'll have to get used to if you intend to be a field archer.

Practice of any sort is a lot more fun and better for you, if someone else shoots with you. Not only is there the pleasant feeling of companionship, but rivalry keeps you on your toes, where shooting by yourself you may grow a little lax. Since archery is a sport appealing to all types of people, you may be able to get someone else in the family to go out and shoot with you. Children are usually excellent instinctive shooters and often make Dad look to his laurels.

Archery is a great sport. It's been called the "sport of man since time began" and that is certainly true. **But you must always remember that a bow and arrow, improperly handled, can be dangerous.** There are only a few rules to be observed when you shoot, but for your own sake, they must be followed.

- Never shoot straight into the air. Neither you nor the people round you can judge where the arrow will fall.
- Never shoot when there are people (or animals, unless game) forward of where you are standing.
- Never, under any circumstances point a drawn bow at another person. An arrow will kill as surely as a bullet.
- Don't shoot unless you know what lies along the arrow's path.
- If any of your arrows crack, smash them and throw them away. A cracked arrow may break on the string and injure you badly.
- In tournament shooting pay attention to the field captain. His word should be law.

If you have trouble remembering the safety rules, think back to the time when man protected himself with his bow. It brought him food and it won him wars. Today's bows are even more dangerous—archery is not a watered-down sport.

Now you're well on your way as an archer. By this time, you must have been firmly bitten by the archery bug and you'll want to meet others of your kind. There are two national associations of archers, both active and vociferous. You'll want to join one, or both.

The organization of the target archers is:
The National Archery Association
Larry Briggs, Secretary
University of Massachusetts
Amherst, Massachusetts

The newer group, the field archers, is:
The National Field Archery Association
John L. Young, Secretary
Box 388
Redlands, California

Both associations will put you in touch with the archery club nearest to you. And in case there is none, both associations conduct contests by mail, so you can shoot against someone else, if only by remote control. Or even better they'll put you in touch with other "loners" and you can form your own group—pair, foursome or club. It's fun and fine practice. •

Photo by Anthony Lane, courtesy Paul Bunyan Bait Co.

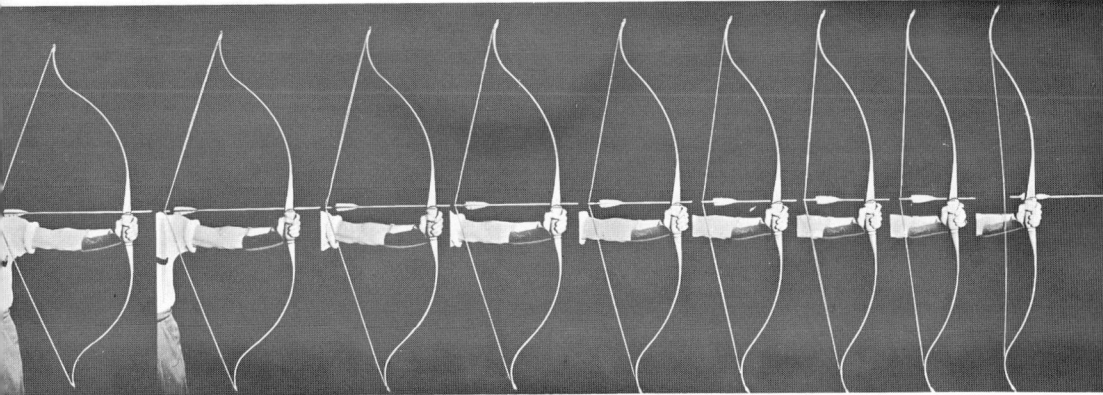

Stroboscopic photo of arrow-release shows good form: bow-arm remains steady, handle loose in hand.

All photos in this chapter are by Hal Kelly. Courtesy Robin Hood Archery Co.

ARCHERY LESSON IN PHOTOS

Three times a national champion and many times winner of sectional as well as state tournaments, Ann Weber Corby here teaches shooting technique.

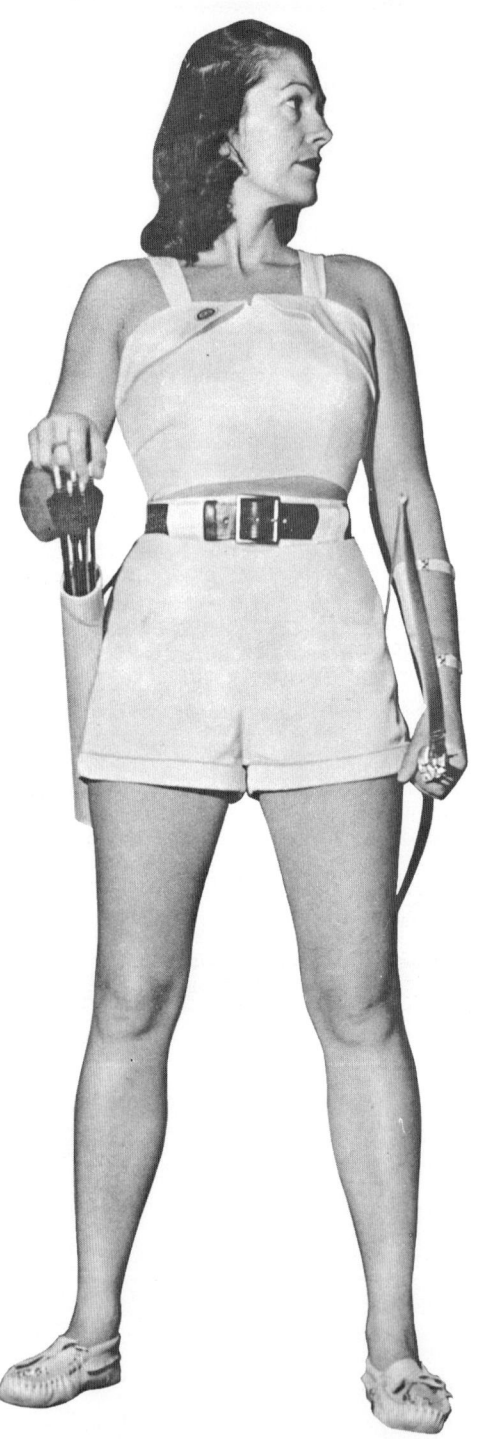

Stance is very important: spread feet well apart with weight of body evenly distributed and straddle shooting line. Study above photo.

Grip bow naturally but not tightly as if it were suitcase handle turned horizontally, then lay arrow along shelf on bow alongside bow-grip and slide it straight back to string, gripping string with first three fingers of hand. Be sure string is well seated in first joints, not fingertips.

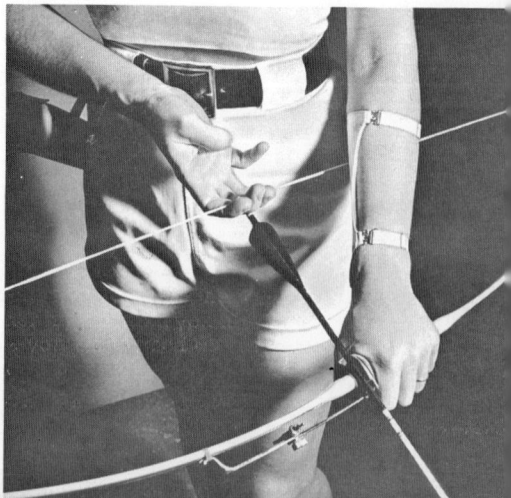

ARCHERY LESSON IN PHOTOS

Keeping body-weight well-distributed on feet slowly raise bow as shown. Body is at right angle to target.

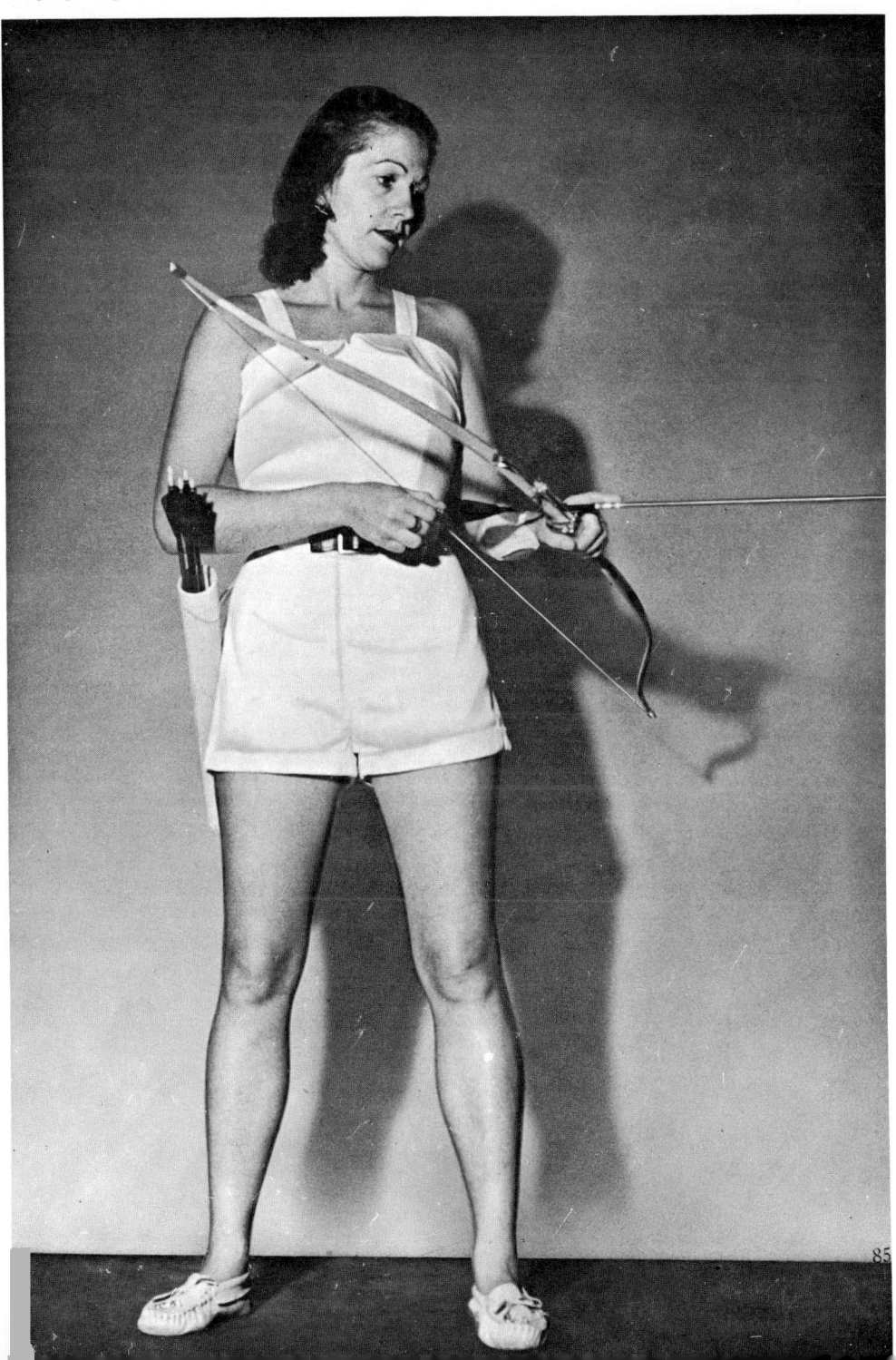

Swing bow to vertical position, extending string-arm directly toward target. Take a deep breath as you draw.

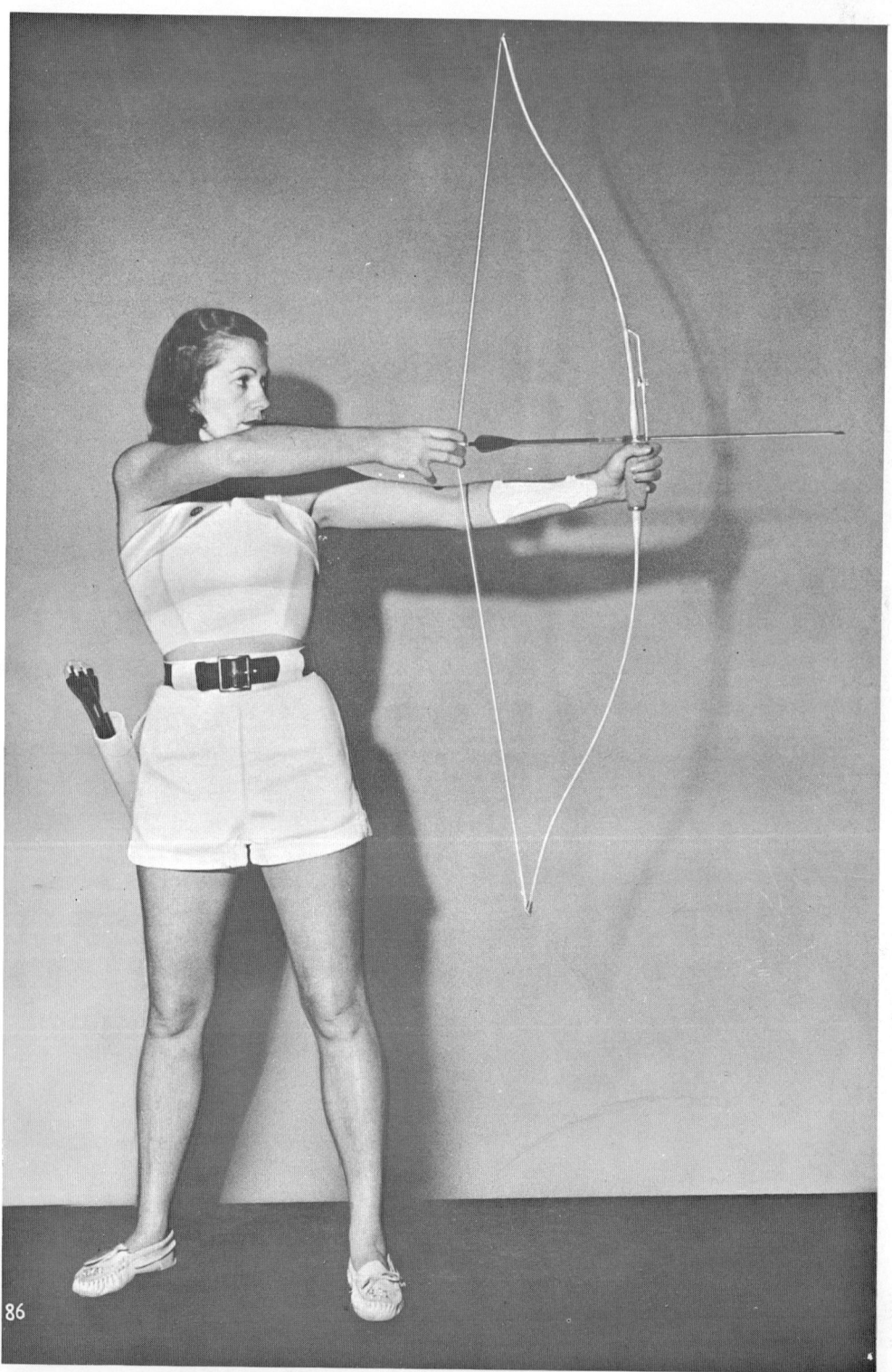

ARCHERY LESSON IN PHOTOS

Draw back evenly, feeling easy rhythm. Keep wrist loose; use back and shoulder muscles. Elbow is out.

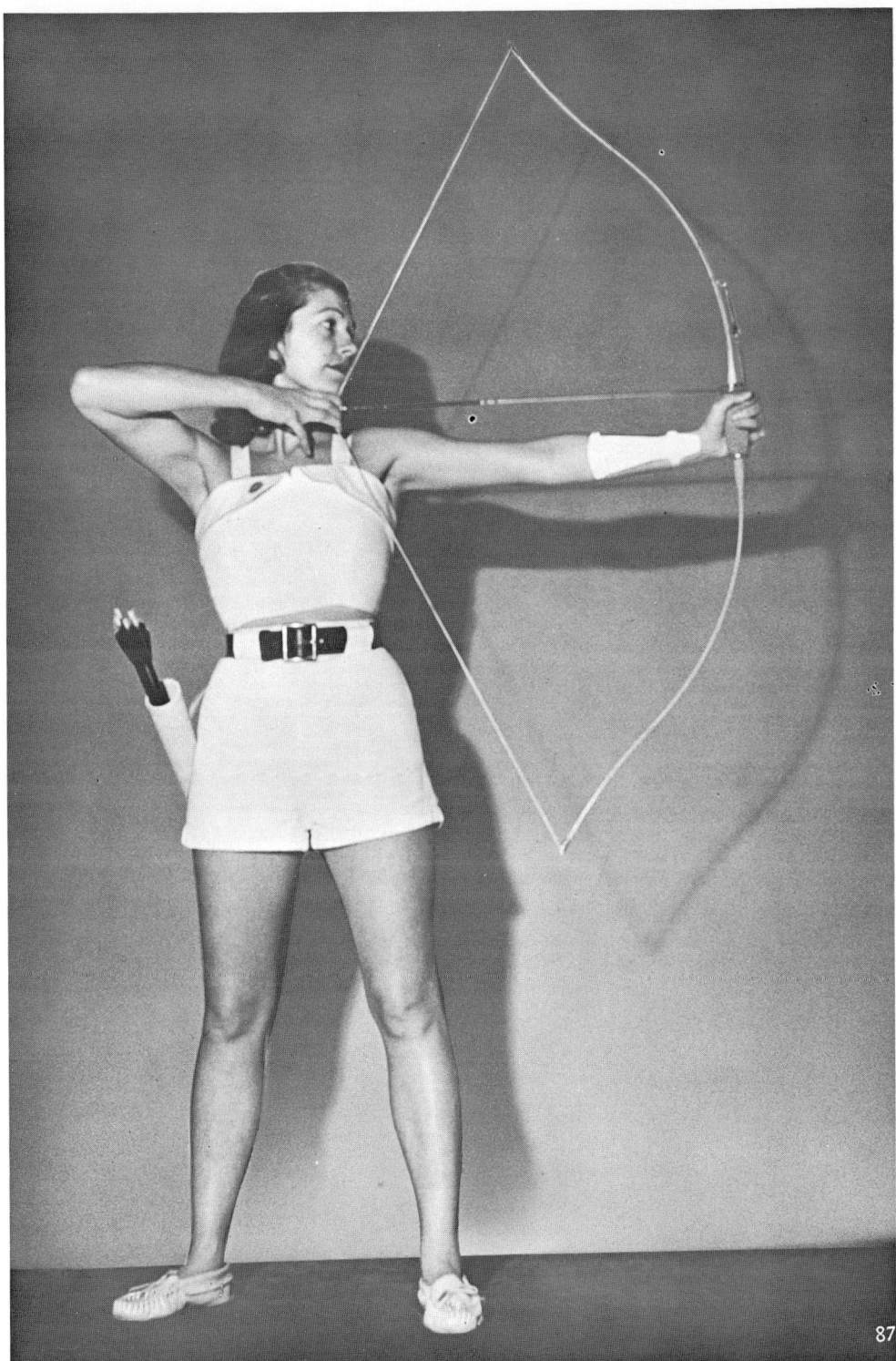

Draw is to "anchor point," or chin center. String should lightly cut across center of nose also, while forefinger is under, against jaw.

ARCHERY LESSON IN PHOTOS

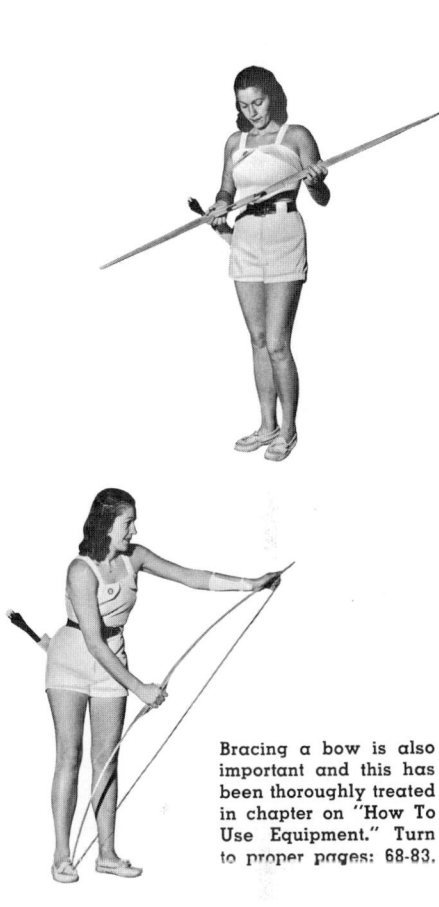

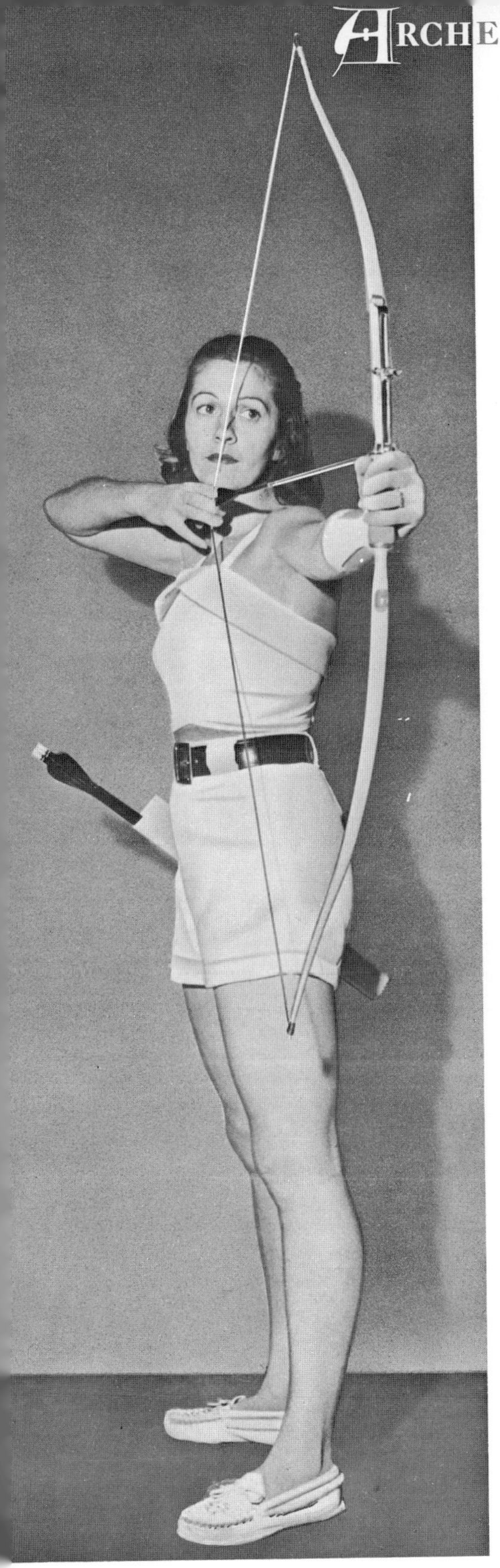

Bracing a bow is also important and this has been thoroughly treated in chapter on "How To Use Equipment." Turn to proper pages: 68-83.

Front view showing how bow is held toward target. Note erect position of body, position of drawing-elbow and straightness of wrists and shoulders.

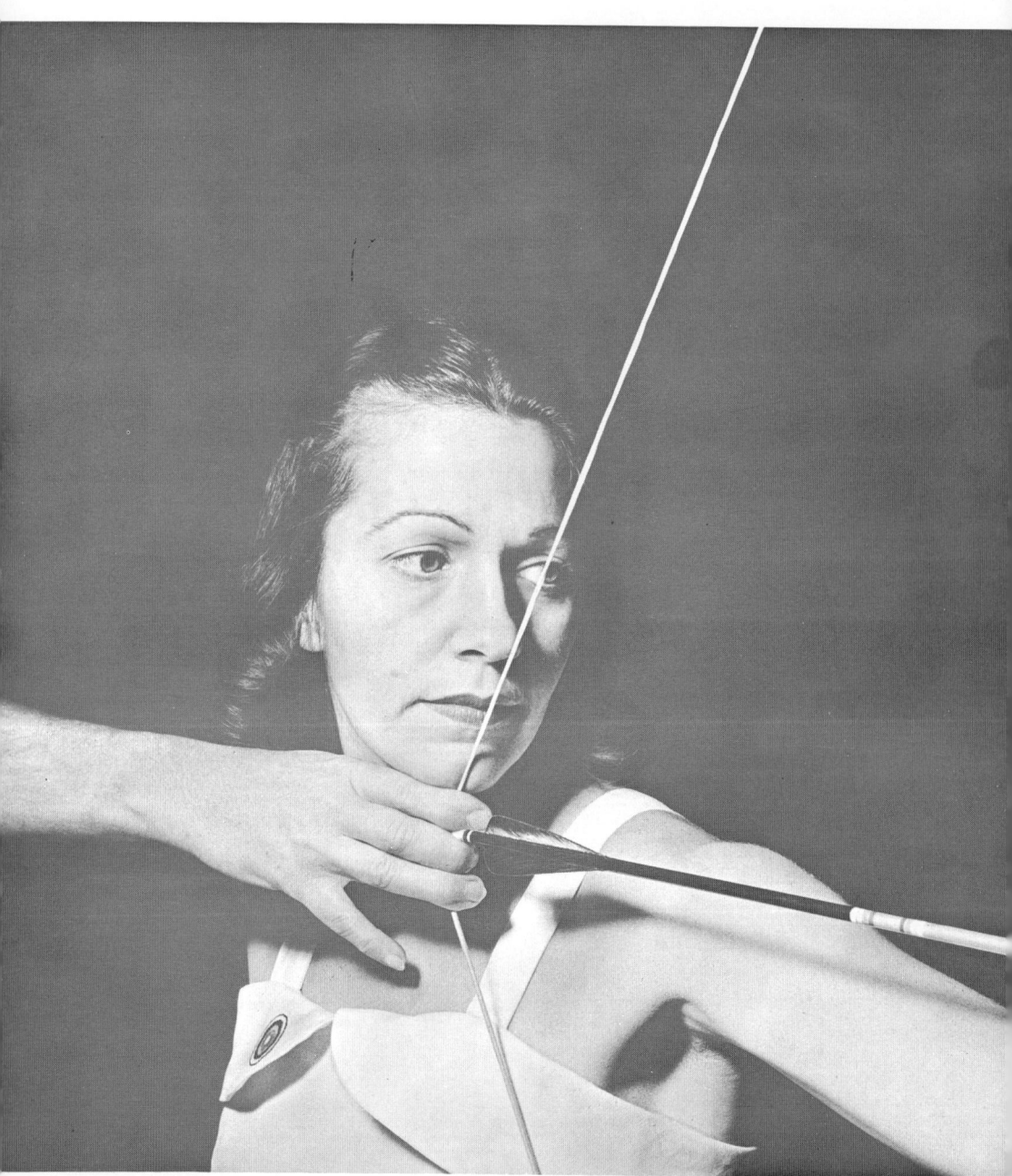

Closeup view of "anchor point." Note how string is drawn firmly into chin, position of forefinger under jawbone, looseness of string in finger joints.

ARCHERY LESSON IN PHOTOS

Most modern archers use a bowsight for aiming. One eye sights through it directly at gold of target center. Again, note straightness of grip.

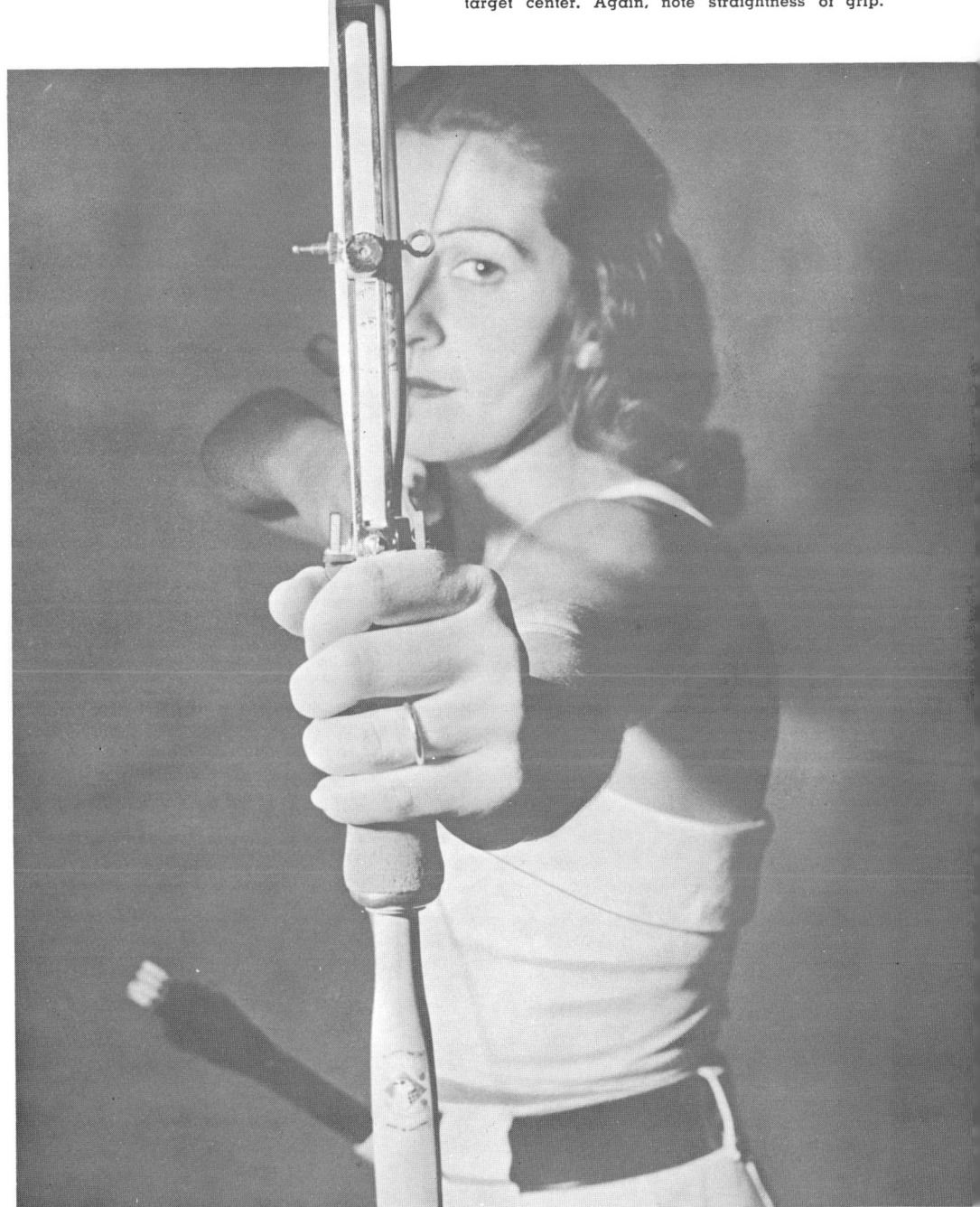

An excellent idea of how bowsight is used is shown here, over archer's shoulder. Note arrow is below sight. Because of flight-parabola, sight may be adjusted for distance, drift.

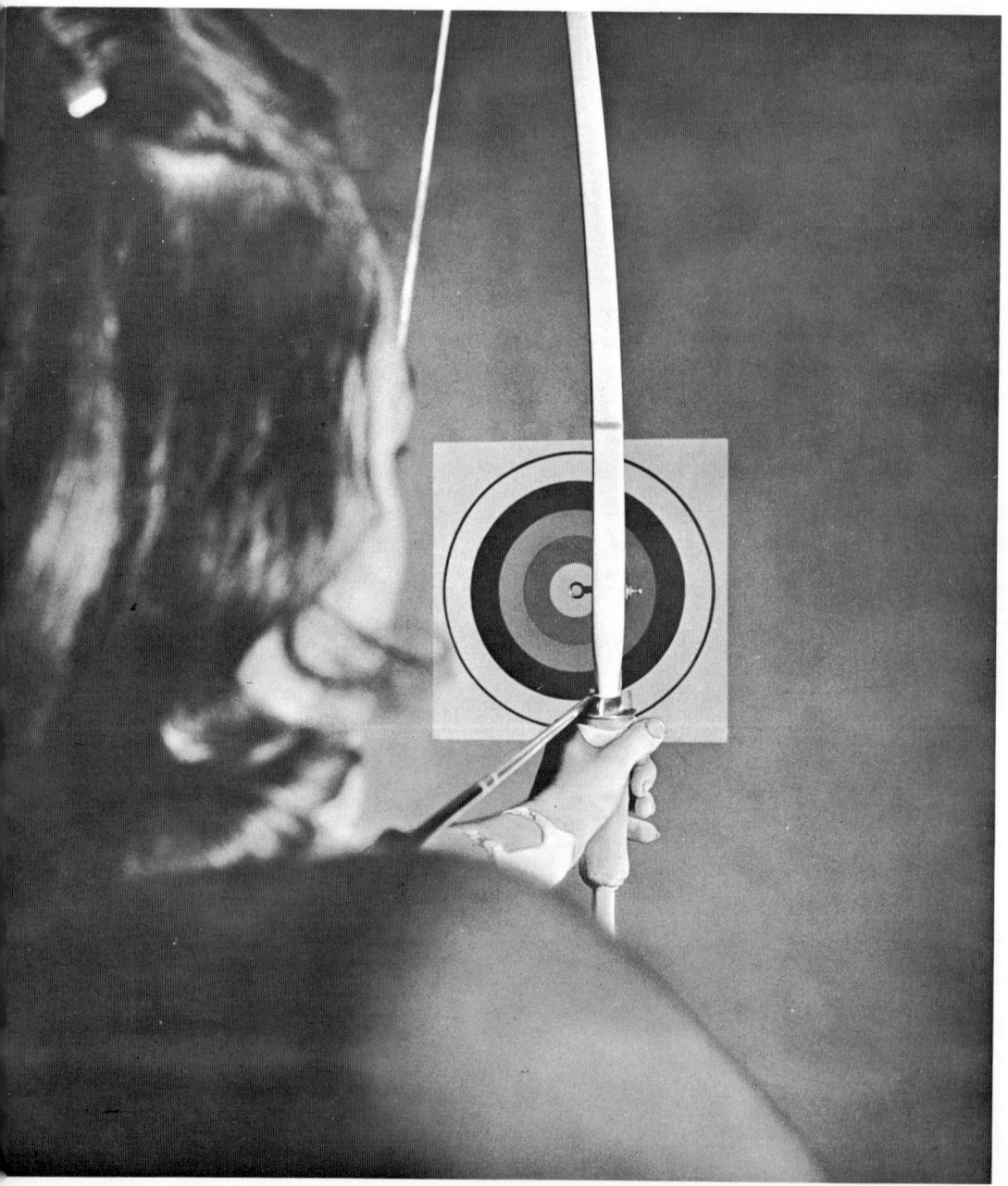

ARCHERY LESSON IN PHOTOS

Arrow is released by letting string roll off relaxed fingers as hand moves directly back to side of neck.

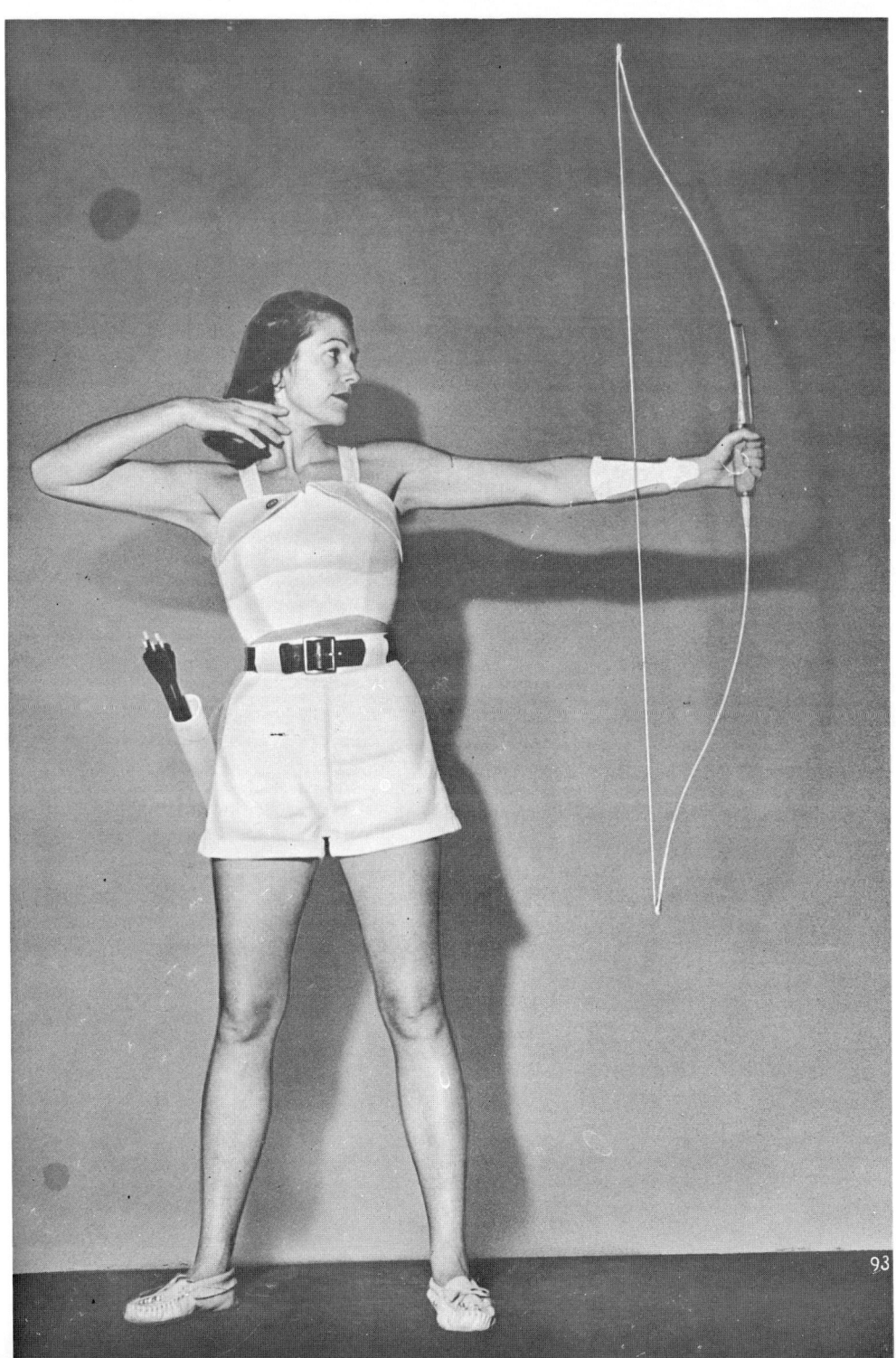

Style of hunting archer differs: various shooting positions are necessary. Bow is held at slight angle.

ARCHERY LESSON IN PHOTOS

From kneeling position bow is held on outside of high knee, but handle grip is same as in target work.

Front view of bow position while kneeling: although bow is held at angle, note firmness and straightness of bow-arm as well as general erectness of the body.

ARCHERY LESSON IN PHOTOS

"Anchor point" in hunting is also different from same thing in target archery: arrow is drawn back until thumb of drawing hand comes firmly up behind the ear.

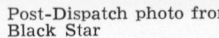
Post-Dispatch photo from Black Star

At right is bow covered with a "bow-sock," which is an attachment of dark, dull cloth that fits over the bow and prevents it from reflecting light that would scare away game.

Archer-hunter must learn to use "protective coloration," same as animals. Dress to blend into surroundings and move quietly when taking aim. Note "bow-sock" on this bow.

Hunting and Seasons

Hunting with a bow and arrow requires the archer to be a better woodsman than the gun-hunter: this chapter gives detailed advice and tips on how to achieve this.

WITH the coming of fall most of us begin to think of hunting. This is the time of year when all the practice with the bow should pay off. Now the hours spent stalking a stump, should, if all goes well, yield dividends.

Successful hunting with a bow, however, is a lot more complicated than just going out for a stroll with a rifle in your hands. By choosing to hunt as an archer, you've put yourself in a strange position. You still want game, perhaps even more than you ever have, and yet you've increased the odds against success immeasurably. For every deer you miss with a rifle, there'll be twenty you'll miss with a bow, or rather there'll be twenty you won't have a chance to hit—we'll assume your practice has made you able to hit what you shoot at.

A good last minute warm-up for the actual hunting season is practice on moving targets. The shots you'll get at game are seldom standing ones and it helps a lot if you are set to loose at something on the move. If you've found companion souls, who, like you, think bow

Hunting and Seasons

Hunting for birds or squirrels takes not only alertness but quick and accurate aiming. Archers should practice carefully in the field in order to achieve speed and skill before going on hunt.

Photo from Three Lions

hunting is the world's best sport, you can rig big mobile targets to run on wires down hillsides. The targets are fine if they look like game, but even that isn't necessary as long as you have the general size and motion. An even simpler form of mobile target practice is to get someone to roll paper or tin plates along sloping ground. It's a sort of trap shooting with a bow and can give you a lot of fun of an afternoon, at the same time that it sharpens your eye for small game. Even this may not be practical if a shooting partner isn't around, and you'll have to find a means of practicing alone. Balloons come to mind in this case, to be used in a variety of ways. Gas filled are the best, but lacking them, just fill your pockets with rubber and your lungs with air and start out. A good breeze is something you need, to give life to your targets. The balloons themselves can be fastened to long strings stretched across paths or glades in the woods, or hidden in grass and bush in more open country. If you really want to get some top notch wing practice in, stand in an open field and let gas filled balloons rise free. They make a fine test of your eye and have the added advantage of teaching you to lead with the bow.

If you do shoot into the air, at balloons or any other moving target, you'd better get a type of arrow called the "floo-floo." Designed originally for birds and squirrels, it has a bushy fletch that twists the vanes round and round. The peculiar fletching gives it a loud whistle as it flies and makes the arrow drop after a maximum range of about sixty yards. Up to that point it is amazingly accurate, if noisy, and its use saves a lot of walking in the field.

Photo from Paul Will

We'll assume you've done all your practicing and are ready to actually hunt. The two are inseparable—it's arrant foolishness for a man to go hunting until he's a good archer. As someone once said, *bow hunting is the pay-off for learning.* You have to take your degree, or graduate from school, before you can take advantage of what you've learned. To go bow hunting without knowing what you're doing is not only a waste of time, but it can be dangerous. If you've just gotten a bow, it's far better to wait for next season, than to go out and go sour on the sport because you weren't ready or capable of enjoying the best moments. You'll also tire out if unpracticed.

You already have most of the tackle you'll need for actual hunting. If you have two bows, the heavier, sturdier one is already earmarked for the hunt. Arrows, *matched to your bow,* should be chosen on the basis of the game you want to hunt. Big broadheads are wasted on cottontails and squirrels. Not only do you stand a good chance of ruining the blade completely but if it hits a tree you can count on a hot half hour getting the metal cut out of the wood. Some manufacturers are making a practice head for field work, of the same weight as a broadhead, which has a thread on the tip for just such cases. This simply means that instead of cutting the head out, you twist and the pile unscrews itself from the tree. Generally, if you're going after small game, use blunts or small broadheads. The blunts will kill by shock, just as well as the blades. For deer, bear, and other big game, use the large broadheads.

A shoulder quiver is almost essential for hunting. The belt quivers hold enough arrows but they have an annoying habit of catching on branches and twigs or snagging on a fence as you go through.

The best plan, before you take to the field is to go over a check list of what you need. Here is a sample:

Bow—check your local game warden on the legal weight limit in your state. Some states have set minimums. See to it that the surfaces of the bow are not highly reflective, a shine can send a deer running minutes before you even see him. Dull finish tape can be used easily, since it is readily removable.

Arrows—a maximum of six are all that are really needed. The only time you might want to carry more will be when you plan to try for more than one kind of game on a single trip.

String—check to see that the string on your bow is in perfect shape. Use a new one if possible and be sure to carry at least one spare, either in your quiver or in the belt pouch.

Bracer or arm-guard and finger protection.

Quiver—if possible, as we've said, use a shoulder quiver. Some archers leave the quiver in camp and carry the arrows in the bow hand, after the style

Photo from Three Lions

Small game can be brought down easily with a blunt-head arrow or a small broadhead. Archer here used much too large a point on a squirrel.

Hunting and Seasons

of the American Indian. Another practice is a bow-quiver, which is fastened on the back of the bow at the handle. Usually holds three arrows, ready to the hand.

- Knife—you often need a good belt knife in the field. The best are sturdy, hold their edge and aren't too long. If you're after big game a well sheathed hatchet is also essential.
- Cheesecloth—necessary only if you're after deer or any other animal with a large body cavity.
- Miscellany—
  Spare strings.
  Spare nocks (plastic type).
  Spare piles.
  File, for keeping a keen edge on the broadheads.
  Wax.
  Spool of silk, for emergency serving.
  Tube of cement for setting nocks and piles in the field.

A quick glance at such a check-list, before you go out, will save you many a headache when you're actually hunting. It's no fun to be caught miles out in the country with some vital piece of equipment missing.

New archers often ask, "Where can I hunt?" The answer is, within reason, almost anywhere you are. There are few if any parts of the country where there isn't game of one sort or another. Certainly, you have to check with your local and state game or conservation authorities before you start, but aside from that there are few limits. Part of the fun of bow hunting is in cooperating with the law. There's sport enough in the hunting that's permitted without setting out to poach.

Pests make just as good targets for the bowman as they do for the gun hunter. There isn't a state in the Union which will stop you from hunting predators, such as crows, coyotes, mountain lion, hawks and the like. The only exceptions to the rule are those animals which are predatory by nature but are classed as fur-bearers and therefore rate protection. Crows are never protected and if you are good enough to match wits with those wily black birds successfully, you'll rate thanks, not only from conservation men but from the farmers, too.

The general rules to follow in looking for a place to hunt is simply to keep your eyes open. Chances are the fields you've used for practice will have game around them. A second point to check is the local newspaper. Many of the larger ones have hunting and fishing editors, who'll be glad to answer your queries. The smaller papers may not have such an editor but chances are someone on the staff will have the information you're after.

The two cardinal rules to remember in

Photo by Judge, courtesy Centaur Archery Co.

At right is wrong way to hunt: never carry field glasses with bow: they might reflect light, make noise. Glasses are excellent, however, for tracking, learning game-habits.

Men below are squirrel hunting with the proper equipment: arrows are blunt-headed and kill by shock instead of penetration. This is much less messy, more fair to game.

Photo from Archery Magazine

looking for hunting country are these:
- Check the state and local game authorities. They will not only give you all the seasons but they themselves are often able to tell you likely places to go.
- Be sure you obtain permission from the land owner before you begin hunting. Few farmers will refuse you the right, but if they do, remember that the cause of the refusal was probably the man who came before you and didn't ask.

After you've looked for a hunting area, you'll want something to shoot at. Again, there's game almost everywhere, and it will be up to you to find it. As we mentioned earlier, predators are almost always "fair game," and so for that matter are the woodchuck and the prairie dog.

The cottontail rabbit, the varying hare and the racy jack rabbit have, among them, a firm hold on most of the country. In many places you'll find two out of the three kinds, and any of them provide good, fast shooting. You may want to hunt them by yourself or you may want to work behind dogs. In either case, your targets will test every bit of your shooting skill.

Rule of thumb, of course, is you can hunt anything with a bow that you can hunt with a gun. Perhaps this isn't quite true. It takes a highly skilled archer to reach up and pull down a Canada goose, but on the pleasant side of the picture, there are a few things you can hunt with a bow the gun-shooter can't touch. In the southern rivers of the United States the big alligators are proving fine targets. Archers in boats go out at night and shoot the huge fish that often run as high as two hundred pounds. In coastal waters archers are hunting game fish and sharks and inland rough fish shooting is becoming popular.

Squirrels are good sport for the bow hunter. They are excellent training for big game hunting since they are so alert the stalker must exercise every precaution to get within bow shot of the chatterers. Since most states protect at least part of their squirrel population, be sure to check your game laws before you go after them.

Upland game birds, in season, are good hunting as are migratory waterfowl, but to take either with a bow requires a degree of skill few of us attain. It may be legal to shoot a cock pheasant on the ground but it still doesn't seem like a really sporting proposition.

We're fortunate in this country to have big game in almost every state. The white-tail deer and his cousins the mule and black-tail deer are found in many areas, both in the East and West. Bear are fairly common and in the West, prong-horn antelope are staging a remarkable recovery, thanks to far-sighted conservation programs. And, of course, there are elk in the Northwest. All in all the bow hunter has a good mixed bag to choose from, starting from almost any point in the nation.

From the standpoint of the biggest annual bag, with gun or bow, the deer is the top big-game animal in the country. Rhode Island is perhaps the only state without at least a few of the graceful animals. Conservationists estimate there are more deer in the United States today than there were when the white men came. The deer have accommodated themselves, by and large, to living with men all around them, and in spite of the terrific toll taken of the herd

Deer and other big game take large broadhead on arrows. Archer here is shown in kind of surroundings that deer prefer: brush country. Note fine form of arrow-draw. Archer is R. L. Mathot, Jr., vice president of Centaur Archery Co., located Glenshaw, Pa.

Photo by Judge, courtesy Centaur Archery Co.

HUNTING AND SEASONS

each year, the total continues to grow. In the East the largest herds are in New England, New York and Pennsylvania. In the Midwest the big concentration is in northern Michigan, Wisconsin and Minnesota. On the West Coast from the Rockies to the sea, deer are universally distributed.

Wily white tails are no respecters of place, however. They pop up in the most unlikely places periodically. In the fall of 1953 a buck suddenly appeared on New York's Staten Island and refused to leave, while on Long Island, practically within sight of the greatest city in the world a special season was declared on deer in 1952. The herd was ravaging farm land to such an extent that the farmers asked for and got special dispensation to kill outside of the normal time limit. A year never goes by without many newspapers reporting deer in the streets of our larger cities. And certain war and postwar influences have served to benefit our deer population.

Primarily deer like fairly open country. While you will find them in deep dense woods, they prefer second-growth or bush country. With World War II, there was a tremendous exodus of farmers away from the land. Farms that had been worked for hundreds of years were abandoned, both because of a lack of help and because industry paid a higher wage scale. The farmland automatically went back into cover,

thousands and thousands of acres of it. With the tremendous increase of second growth, the deer flourished and continue to flourish. There are many areas over the country that had no deer fifteen years ago, where the deer hunter traveled hundreds of miles for the season—today the deer are actually thick. The situation will continue for a while, at least. Two things may stop it—if the land is put under cultivation again and the natural cover is destroyed, or, if the second growth is allowed to grow more, the deer will be forced to seek other areas. Conservationists feel we now have all the deer this so-called "marginal land" will support, in fact, in some regions the deer population has risen to the point where it has been necessary to declare open season on both sexes to prevent overcrowding and the resultant starvation.

Hunting the deer varies with the land. It is impossible to tell you how to hunt deer in the rocky canyon country of the Southwest and have you expect to apply the same specific information to hunting in the Maine woods. The two techniques, each ideally suited to its own locale, are simply not interchangeable. But there are certain principles which are unvarying, in any region and for any game.

Know your country. Hunting in unknown country is a matter of luck, not of skill. The most skillful archer, or gun-

Al Gigler, Ambridge, Pa. archer, first learned to stalk, then spent many days practicing in field: it paid off during antler-less deer season in Pa.

Photo by Hal. H. Harrison from Monkmeyer

G. Judd, another archer-hunter, stopped this buck with a broadhead during the regular deer season for bowmen. Most states demand minimum heads.

Photo by Archery Magazine

Photos on these two pages by Three Lions

Real test of an archer's skill—and nerve—is hunting the wild Russian boar. This animal weighs from 200 to 600 pounds, has razor-sharp tusks. Boar photographed here was found in South Carolina mountains.

hunter, goes in with two strikes against him, when he hunts unknown territory. If it is at all possible, spend a few days, before you start to hunt, in a careful survey of the area. Move around, watching for trails, for signs, for prevailing winds. Learn the location of feeding and drinking places and mark probable bedding spots.

Know your game. When you pit yourself against big game, using a bow, you are giving odds to your quarry. Your only possible chance of success is to familiarize yourself with the animals in question to the best of your ability. Learn to track, learn to tell from the trail what the sex of the animal is, how fast it traveled and if it was just out for a stroll or on the run.

Learn to move in the open. Many of us, cooped up in cities, find it hard to move around in the open, with any ease. You have to learn to do that, if you want game. The successful hunter, east or west, north or south, is the man who blends in with his surroundings, who becomes a stealthily moving part of the scenery. If your foot breaks a twig, or kicks a loose stone, your game is gone before you ever see it. The wind and sun can either be your allies or your enemies in the open. Train yourself to really use your eyes—something we often forget to do in everyday living. That flick of motion may be an animal's ear and that patch of light may be a leg.

Learn to shoot from any position. Learn that most of your shots won't be straight away. Learn to shoot from behind a tree, without exposing yourself. Teach yourself to shoot from a crouch, kneeling or even lying flat on the ground. Often you may have your only shot at game from under a clump of brush—where you have to hold the bow parallel to the ground. Don't get to the point where your accuracy is lost because you aren't in the position you trained with—use them all. Think of the most ridiculous and seemingly impossible shots and then practice them, until it becomes a second part of your nature to shoot from any angle, at any target.

Specifically, when you go to hunt, choose

HUNTING AND SEASONS

your clothing with care and learn to regulate your life to the life around you. Dr. Pope, the great hunting archer, had as a mentor an Indian named Ishi. Under his tutelage, Pope became the first modern bow hunter, whose successful exploits served to arouse so much interest in the sport. Ishi, who was the last survivor of his tribe, brought to Pope all of the legendary woodcraft of the native Americans. While the Indian was not a great archer in the sense of high scoring on a target, he was a superb stalker, able to move in on his quarry like a shadow, able to kill from extremely close range. Ishi once told Pope that white men moved through the woods like horses, smelled like horses, but didn't have as much sense as a horse.

As far as game is concerned, we stink. Our odor, by itself, is strong and rank to animal nostrils, and we thoughtlessly augment it with the many stinks of civilization. Gasoline, coal smoke, alcohol, tobacco and strong soaps all form an overlay on our natural body smell so it is a wonder we ever see game unless we exercise every

precaution. When you start to hunt, try to wear clothing which is not only unobtrusive to the eye, but to the nose as well. Since many states today have special bow seasons set up, there is no need for the bow hunter to wear the flaming scarlet of tradition. Game may or may not be color blind, but it is a definite fact they notice both red and white as well as certain shades of bright blue. Your clothes should be soft enough to prevent rattling on the brush and yet not so soft as to cling and stick to every obstacle. They should be warm without being bulky and they should be clean. If you have a chance, place the outfit you'll wear on the actual hunt between layers of pine boughs, or any native branches which will give it a certain natural smell. Don't sleep in the clothes you'll hunt in—this may save a little packing, but on the other hand it may cost you a good shot. Cut down on your tobacco or stop it altogether if you can. Eliminate as much meat as possible from your diet—all meat eaters, and man is one, have a killer smell to them that animals are quick to recognize. Bathe before you start, carefully and thoroughly, but don't use soap. You're trying to take scent away, not add to it.

Walk quietly. We go through life on heels and our feet strike heel first. The good stalker goes through the woods or brush with flat soles, his toes striking the ground first. They feel out the land in front of him, warning him to draw back before the fallen limb cracks or the stone rolls. The ideal foot gear for hunting is the traditional Indian moccasin, with a self-sole, limber and soft. It's the closest thing in the world to going barefoot. But it has a disadvantage in that it is so soft that rock and sand will cut it to bits in a short space of time. So if you are going to hunt in rocky, rough country a pair of tennis shoes makes an acceptable substitute. There are even extremists who put straps of adhesive tape across the soles of their bare feet, but it's not a method for hunting in snow, whereas either the moccasins or the tennis shoes will do well, with lots of snow on the ground. If you're afraid of getting your feet wet, just don't bother to go hunting. And don't wear great harsh leather boots, with hard soles and heels. It's almost impossible to move in the woods with them without advertising your coming for a hundred yards. Wear a soft shoe and walk with

Boar-hunt starts with well-trained dogs baying quarry. No archer in right mind hunts boar alone.

Boar is laid low finally with a broadhead in brain after long chase that cost several dogs.

the toes slightly in, hitting the ground first.

Hunting the white tail is usually done in one of two ways, still-hunting and driving. Either way will yield game—and some areas favor one, some the other. The still hunter can ply his art under any circumstances, alone or with companions. The drive is a communal effort. Both methods are used by gun-hunters as well as bowmen, but as always the bow-hunter must bring more skill to his practice.

Driving. It always takes more than one man to drive-hunt. There may only be two in the party but more often there are from six to a dozen. Driving presupposes a thorough knowledge of the area and the game in it. It also is largely dependent on certain types of terrain. Essentially, the hunters are posted at stands or watches, while the drivers go away and drive toward the men on watch.

The group splits itself into standers and drivers and the standers are posted. Since it is a cooperative method of hunting, it's always best for a captain to be chosen, who should know the land best. He must pick stands for the hunters, so placed as to allow free shooting in areas where the game will pass. Fire lanes, draws, timber trails and natural glades must all be used as well as natural obstacles to prevent breakouts as drivers herd the game to the watchers.

The watchers must be quiet, and as motionless as humanly possible. The slightest sound—a cough, a cleared throat or an off-key whistle spoils the drive. *And you have to stand still.* If a man moves around he's lost. A deer, coming along the trail, may not see a motionless man—may, as some hunters maintain, mistake him for a dead tree. But the bow hunter, who must shoot at close range, is forced to move before he can shoot. Therefore, he has to stay out of sight. In many areas where driving is often practiced, blinds are built to accommodate the watcher along the trails.

Perhaps the hardest part about posting a group of men on stands is the wind. The posts must be chosen so the deer are driven, with the wind, never into it. If driven deer catch the scent of the watchers ahead of them they will double back through the driving line, or off to one side or the other, rather than face the danger

Fishing with bow is another sport that offers excitement and a real test of "fisherman's" skill.

Photo by Hollyman from Monkmeyer

About 50 ft. of heavy nylon casting line is tied to arrow. Reels can be made or bought to fit bow.

Post-Dispatch Photo from Black Star

Hunting and Seasons

they are sure to sense ahead of them.

The drivers, working in a rough line, should cover the area to be driven as completely as possible. No patch of thick bush should be skipped, for the biggest bucks often lie up in them. A great deal of noise isn't necessary, but some helps to push the deer along ahead. Some old drivers, with years of woodcraft behind them will come through the bush almost as silently as the hunter, but the deer move ahead of them. Don't take much tackle with you, if you're driving. You'll be going through much thicker brush than you would ordinarily and it's easy to snag or break equipment.

Watchers on stand should bear in mind that if they are right handed, they should be on the right side of the trail, glade or path, and if left handed, vice versa. Keep as low as possible and don't stand up to shoot. A deer may not be able to get out of the way of a bullet, but an archer, rising and drawing gives the quarry too much time to make a getaway. Wait until the deer is abreast of your stand before you shoot. You give yourself a much broader target, and since the deer is probably looking ahead rather than to the side, any slight movement on your part is less likely to make him change direction and speed. *And don't make any noise.* A deer that's broadside to you at thirty yards can hear an arrow going back across the bow without any trouble and, keyed up by the danger, will be gone in a flash. Be sure the arrows ride across the arrow plate, and be doubly sure that it's a quiet type of plate.

Still hunting. Here is the supreme test of the archer's skill, not only with his equipment, but with woodcraft. If you take a deer by stalking, you will have earned your master's degree. It is an art, calling for every bit of practice and every bit of knowledge at your command.

If possible, get to your hunting area two or three days before you plan to start. Those hours will be well invested in checking feeding grounds, watering spots and bed areas. If you have a chance you should have done these things earlier, but

Although this bow-fisherman is using a regular fletched arrow with hooked point, much bow fishing is done without feathers on arrow, since distance of shot is usually not great. Many states allow fishing.

Photo by Lervis from Monkmeyer

107

Post-Dispatch photos from Black Star

In Missouri (and other states) gar-fishing is encouraged. The gar is a predatory rough fish that game wardens do not like. Night-fishing for the gar is a favorite sport of midwestern archers, who use lights.

if not, this pre-hunt period will give you a chance to do the "spade work." Select your campsite and get your equipment in top shape. Air your clothing, and do all the last minute things which might have been forgotten.

Deer are among the smartest animals in the world, at least when it comes to protecting themselves. They are on their home grounds and the odds are all with them when you go after them, *with a gun or with a bow*. And *you increase their odds* when you hunt with the bow. Hunting requires preparation and planning and there is no better way to waste your time than to go blithely off, hoping to pick up a trophy.

After you've selected your campsite, your first step, if you are in unfamiliar territory is to get up as high as you can and look over the surrounding countryside. A pair of binoculars provides immeasurable help in such a survey, but don't use them when you're actually hunting. The reflection of sunlight on the lenses will spook game, just when you think you're safely out of sight.

Look for old orchards and buckwheat fields, in the East and Middle West. In the dry country of the Southwest, look for the patches of green which will indicate spots the deer may come to feed. Check along stream banks and the shores of lakes and ponds for signs indicating where the animals come to water. *Explore—but explore carefully*. In many places you'll cut well-marked trails that the game use regularly, either going to feed, or to drink. Examine them carefully—your lessons in tracking will serve you in good stead here. Move along the trails, but parallel, not on the tracks themselves. And above all, move slowly. In any type of terrain, it's well worth the time spent to move slowly and softly. The next glade, the next draw, the next hill may have game on or in it. Watch the ground in front of you carefully and

Hunting and Seasons

This archer has just speared a large gar. Many archers also fish salt water, from shore or boats.

Photo courtesy Stuart Wilson, Jr., president N. Y. State Field Archery Association

Arnold Haugen, Lansing, Mich., hit fox in leg with first arrow, finished it off with a second.

then walk without breaking brush. *Stop every once in a while* and squat down, to look around you from that angle. *Check your back trail*—deer have been known to follow a hunter.

Remember that deer move about during the night, and if there is much moonlight, they feed a great deal in the dark hours as well. During the day, they lie up, usually on a hillside, where they can command a view of their back trail and where the wind will warn them of danger.

One of the surest ways to insure bagging a deer is to locate a herd and follow its movements for a day or two. If you can possibly use the time, it is one of the best ways to success. Go through the same exploratory moves and try to spot your quarry. Then follow their daily habits, always bearing in mind that animals are by and large creatures of habit. Stay out of sight, and out of smell. Don't in any way alarm them, but keep the closest possible check on their movements. Here again field glasses are invaluable.

Once you've learned when and where the herd is liable to be at any time, you're much better prepared to hunt. If you can judge that they will drink at an approximate hour every morning, you can be safely in position, with the wind in your favor when they come to water. If you know a particular patch of browse they favor, or a grove of beechnuts to which they're partial, and the time, you're that much ahead of the game. With a variety of spots to choose from you have the added advantage of being able to place yourself to your best advantage, with both the wind and the sun in your favor. The sun is just as hard on an animal's eyes as it is on yours and with the wind in your direction and the sun at your back, you increase your chances.

Moving around over the country, you may sometimes see a doe, or a group of

Photo courtesy Stuart Wilson, Jr., president N. Y. State Field Archery Association
Howard Hill, world-famous champion archer, went out after really big game in RKO movie on Africa.

does and fawns, but no buck. If that happens and you're in position to shoot, just stand still and wait. The buck is even cagier than his mate and often enough, he'll lurk back in the brush until he sees how the rest of the family makes out in open country. More than once a doe and fawn will step leisurely across a road and be out of sight before the old man of the tribe will put his lordly head in sight.

There is one primary rule, one cardinal tenet to be observed with wounded game—*it's up to you to finish the job.* Beside that simple statement everything else fades away. Once you've drawn blood, it's up to you and you alone to dispatch your quarry, as rapidly as possible. The man or woman who wounds game and makes no attempt to finish it off is the worst criminal in the woods and fields. The only place in the world the rule isn't followed is in Africa on safari, and there it's the job of the professional white hunter.

The rule, which is instinctive with the true sportsman, is just as true for a wounded rabbit as it is for a wounded elephant. It is his or her responsibility—come rain or shine, sleet or snow, hell or high water. In this sense, the bow hunter has an advantage over the man with the rifle in many cases. Shooting from as close a range as he usually does, the archer usually knows when he's hit his animal. And remembering that the arrow kills by bleeding, while the bullet kills by shock, if at all, he has an easier job, by and large, when it comes to following the track of the wounded game. Often enough, small game will die from shock with an arrow and many times they are pinned to the ground

hUNTING AND SEASONS

Photo courtesy Stuart Wilson, Jr., president N. Y. State Field Archery Association
Fred Bear finally bagged a big one in Ontario, Canada, but he had to track bull moose along river for days.

by the shaft—if you're using small broadheads. If not, they leave a blood trail that the uninitiated can follow easily. With big game, it's a different story.

Using the deer again, as an example, let's look at what may happen. If you hit your deer anywhere in the chest area, there's little to worry about. The buck will probably have dropped his flag down fast and taken a leap up in the air before he hightailed it out of sight. If your hit was at all clean, and you should be able to tell—he has only a little way to go before he drops dead. The steel of the broadhead, severing the great blood vessels of the area will cause complete hemorrhage within minutes. All you have to do is sit down and wait before you begin to follow the trail.

That wait is essential, if you're to get your buck with the least amount of trouble. A badly wounded animal will not run far unless it knows that it's being chased. They go a little way and lie down, there to bleed quietly to death. So sit down and take your time—being just as quiet as though you were still hunting. Your buck may be just around the next bend in the trail, listening for any sound of pursuit and should he hear you, walking around, whistling or talking, he'll get up and go, wound or no wound. When enough time has passed, usually a minimum of a half hour, get after him. If he isn't dead from the bleeding by then he'll be so sick and sore and *stiff* that he'll be unable to go far or fast.

Look around then for the arrow with which you hit him. Unless it lodged in muscle clump or bone, the chances are it will have completely penetrated the ani-

Photos on these two pages courtesy Stuart Wilson, Jr., president N. Y. State Field Archery Association

mal. You should also be able to tell exactly where the buck stood when you drove at him. If he didn't bleed at the exact spot, his leap will have dug divots in the ground which can be readily spotted. From the trail you can tell a lot about the animal and its condition. The blood, and there'll be a lot of it, (more than with a gun wound) will be an indicator of where you hit and how hard. The distance between tracks will tell you how much jump the animal could muster as he went. If you hit him in or near the heart he'll leave bright, clear blood at about belly height from the ground. If it was a lung hit, there will have been big blood vessels cut and the buck will be spraying blood from his nostrils as he goes so the whole trail will be spattered

W. B. Wescott, Boston, Mass., bagged this one in Algona County, Mich. Note special bow-quiver.

K. Knickerbocker, Chicago, also bagged his buck in Mich., using a 2-edged broadhead as shown.

with frothy clots. A stomach hit will be dark, the blood almost black and if he's been feeding you may find bits from the stomach along the way.

If all goes well and you've wounded him badly, you'll have no trouble. But there are cases where the wound is so slight that the deer kept going or there are others, when he was badly wounded but something kept him spooked so he never had a chance to stop and stiffen up. In either instance, it'll be up to you to follow the trail —follow it to the bitter end. Every bit of technique you know, or have heard of, will serve you well here. If you lose the trail, you just have to circle from the last point where you are sure you had it until you cut it again. If night comes, mark furthest point and be ready to come back the next day to take the trail up again. The only excuse for abandoning the trail, ever, is if you have personally satisfied yourself you only grazed the animal and that it will make a complete recovery. If the slightest doubt remains in your mind, no matter how hard the trail is, it's up to you to keep after him until you come up.

One archer got a chest shot at a big black bear and spent the next three and a half days following the wounded beast. When he finally caught up the bear was nearly dead from hunger and weakness. But at the same time he was nearly out of his mind from the pain of the wound, and had some stray hiker come near him, he would certainly have attacked. That, however, is not our prime consideration. It's the thought of leaving a wounded animal to die of thirst or starvation, which makes us go on and on, along trails which may often be mere suggestions.

Only one other set of circumstances may come up which will keep you from tracking. If the weather changes, bringing rain or snow to completely obliterate any vestige of sign, then it is forgivable to abandon the trail—but otherwise *never*.

After you've made your kill, there's still the problem of what to do with it. No one hunts game without wanting it, either for food or for a trophy. While bow hunters aren't essentially meat hunters, there's something about the flavor of game that's fallen to your bow which is extra special. Small game is simple to handle and we'll look at it from an over-all standpoint. If you've been using blunt points and depending on shock to kill, you should slit the throat as soon as you get to the spot. When the blood has drained out you can either put the game in a game pocket as is, or dress it out to a certain extent. Make a slit in the skin from the breastbone down to the tail, taking care not to cut deeply enough to puncture the intestines. Reach in and remove the whole intestinal tract and then take out the lungs, heart and other bits in the upper part of the body. When you take the intestines out, be sure to get the gall bladder out whole and if you should break it, put the whole thing in running water as fast as possible, or else your meat will be spoiled. With some animals there are glands of one sort or another, which must be handled with care to avoid spoilage. When you have gotten this far, run water into the body cavity and then dry it out with a soft cloth. Wrap the carcass in cloth and put it in your game pocket or knapsack.

If you've never cleaned game, your first experience may be a little on the unpleasant side. But you'll have to do the job or the meat will spoil. One thing the bow hunter is often saved is the bleeding of his prize. Since most arrow wounds kill by hemorrhage, most of our prizes are already bled white when we get to them. In the event you think the animal still needs bleeding, tug the carcass around so that the head is downhill and slit the throat. If not, you're ready to begin eviscerating him.

The first step is to get the head up as far as possible and the hindquarters down. Most of the time you'll be able to take advantage of the slope of the land but if not, you may have to use a tree. Next turn the animal over so that it is lying on its back and then slit the wall of the stomach from the breastbone to the vent. Use a good sharp knife for the work—and it's important that the knife be good and sharp. You don't need a machete, but whatever steel you use should take and hold an edge that will shave hair.

The cut you made down the belly should be deep enough to penetrate the stomach wall, but under no circumstances should you slice into any part of the intestinal tract. When the incision reaches the rectum cut a circle around the area. Being very careful, pull the rectum and the attached gut out a few inches from the body, where you tie it off.

Some people next take a hand axe or hatchet and open the chest cavity by hacking the ribs free of the breastbone on one side. Another method is to slit the diaphragm with your knife and work your hand up inside. There you cut the gullet and bring it, still attached to the stomach, outside of the body. It is largely a matter of choice in picking which method you'll use. However, if you are hunting in weather that is quite warm, or in warm country, the opening of the rib cage with a hatchet seems much better, since it allows the meat to cool more rapidly.

At any rate, once you've opened the lung area, your next step will be to loosen the stomach in its bed and separate the liver. Fried deer liver is a delicacy, dear to the hunter's heart. Wrap it in soft cloth and lay aside while you finish dressing the carcass.

Turn the body on its side and the entire mass of viscera should roll out. At this point you remove the bladder, pinching it off above the cut and being careful not to allow urine to contaminate any of the meat. You may or may not want to remove the sex glands after the bladder's been taken out. Some states want all evidence of the animal's sex retained until the trophy is checked by a warden. Others don't.

Your animal is now ready to be brought into camp. Most of our North American big game can be carried by one man, especially after it has been bled and gutted. Sling it over your shoulders with the legs forward and you're ready to walk. At the campsite the animal should be hung from a tree, head up, so as to allow any body fluids to drain off. Also a good plan calls for placing a straight stick across the body cavity, spreading the walls as far apart as they'll go. If you've opened the chest, two sticks should be used. This lets the air flow freely through the body and hastens cooling. The last stage is to drape the hanging animal with cheesecloth, to keep out blowflies. Some hunters wipe the carcass with a blood-soaked cloth to form a hard crust which will prevent the blowflies from laying their eggs, but the use of cheesecloth is just as easy, especially if you plan on quartering the kill as soon as it's cool. If you're going to be in camp for any length of time and the weather continues to be warm, take your animal and wrap it carefully in several thicknesses of cloth during the day as insulation against sun and heat.

One mistake many inexperienced hunters make is to load game across the fenders of their cars. Usually the idea seems to be that they want to dash home to show family and friends what happy nimrods they are. The only bad part about it is that the heat of the engine is, more often than not, sufficient to spoil the meat, especially if John Hunter hasn't gutted his kill and allowed it to cool. Let the neighbors admire your prowess after you get home, not on the way. •

Photo by Judge
Courtesy Centaur Archery Co.

HUNTING AND SEASONS

On the following pages of this chapter is a listing of game laws and licensing costs for bow-hunters in every state of Union that permits such hunting. Since laws change, it is wise to write game commissions.

Bow Hunting Seasons and License Costs

It is impossible to tell what the bow and arrow season will be in any given area on any given year, ahead of time. The information listed below is the latest available, but subject to change by the various state agencies. Before you start to hunt, be sure that you obtain, from the state involved, a complete and up-to-date listing of the information. Since most hunting is done in the fall, the game commissions usually establish their current seasons somewhere between the months of May and September. In the event the information is not available, you can get what you want by writing to the National Field Archery Association at Redlands, California. The NFAA has been very active in obtaining special rights for bow hunters and their divisional and state representatives work hand in hand with the various game commissions.

ALABAMA

To date there have been no special archery laws. A hunting license is needed. State license: $3. Non-Resident: $25. There have been special hunting seasons in the past, in the Bankhead National Forest. Hunting gars with a bow is allowed in the Gulf of Mexico and in impoundments of the Tennessee River. For further information write to the Department of Conservation, Division of Game and Fish, Montgomery, Ala.

ARIZONA

There has been a special eight day bow-hunting season in the Kiabab Forest. You need to be a part of the Kiabab Cooperative Hunting Agreement ($5), holding a regular license to participate. Otherwise, bow hunting is legal and accepted at any time during gun season throughout the state. Resident hunting license: $2.50. Non-Resident Big-Game: $50. Non-Resident Small Game: $10. Bows must have a minimum pull of fifty pounds and broadheads must have a width of at least one inch.

ARKANSAS

The Arkansas Bow Hunters Association is very active and can give you full and up-to-date information. A resident can use a bow for hunting, if he obtains a permit to accompany his regular license. Non-residents must pay $6 for a permit, which allows them to hunt deer and wild turkey. If they are successful, they must then purchase a transportation tag, fee: $20.00. There is usually a pre-season period for bow hunters on both deer and turkey. For further information contact either the Bow Hunters Association, Hall Building Annex, Little Rock, or the Arkansas Game and Fish Commission, Little Rock. Bows must draw forty pounds or better and the broadheads must be ⅞" wide.

CALIFORNIA

California has, in the past, had two special seasons for deer hunting with bow and arrow. Use of bow and arrow is also legal during regular hunting season, but if the archer has hunted in the special seasons he may not hunt in the regular period. Resident license: $3. Resident deer tag: $1. Non-Resident archery deer tag: $10. In inland waters only carp may be hunted with the bow. Regulations state broadheads must be ⅞" wide for big game.

COLORADO

Colorado law has not specified a special bow season, but areas have been set aside for pre-seasonal bow hunting. Archers can also hunt during regular gun season. Resident licenses, deer: $7.50; elk: $10. Non-Resident deer: $40; elk $50. Minimum bow weight allowable 40 pounds; broadheads must be one inch wide.

HUNTING AND SEASONS

CONNECTICUT
Use of the bow and arrow is legal during gunning seasons. Special permits are issued to archers. Licenses: Resident: $4.35; non-Resident: $11.35; deer tag: $2.35.

DELAWARE
Little bow hunting has been done in Delaware, but to date, the use of archery is legal. Licenses: Resident: $2.25; non-Resident: $15.50.

FLORIDA
Bow hunting legal during all game seasons. Fish hunting is not legal. Licenses: Resident (county): $2.00; (state) $7.50; non-Resident: $26.50; 10-Day $11.50.

GEORGIA
Bow hunting legal during all regular game seasons. For the past few years special bow hunts have been conducted under direction of the U. S. Forest Service and the Chattahoochee Bowmen in the Chattahoochee National Forest. Special license for this hunt: $5.00. Non-Resident license: $5. Regulations require bows and arrows capable of killing deer.

IDAHO
Idaho has recognized bow hunting by the establishment of a special area reserved for the use of archers. This area is set aside by the game commission and is subject to change. Licenses: Resident hunting: $4. Non-Resident: $50 for first species taken, $25 for each additional.

ILLINOIS
Since there is no big game season in the state, there is no big game bow hunting. Otherwise bow hunting is legal for all small game subject to same regulations as gunning. A special bow hunting season has been set up in the past for rough fish. Licenses: Resident: $2. Non-Resident: $15.

INDIANA
Does not allow hunting of fish with a bow. Archers are allowed special tolerance in that they may hunt on Sunday, which is denied gun hunters. In 1951 first deer season in 50 years was declared—8,600 acres were set aside for bow hunters. Season may be repeated at discretion of game commission. For current details write to Department of Conservation, State of Indiana, Indianapolis, Indiana. Licenses: Resident: $2. Deer: $5. Non-Resident: $15.50.

IOWA
No big game may be taken with a bow, nor any fish. Resident license fee is to be $1.50. Non-Resident is the same as in the archers home state, but not less than $5.

KANSAS
Bow and arrow are recognized as legal weapons and may be used on any game which it is legal to take with a gun. There are no special reserves and no special seasons for archers. No big game hunting.

KENTUCKY
Bow hunting legal during gun season and in the past the state game commission has established pre-seasons for archers. Fish that may be taken by gigging (spearing), may also be taken with bow during gigging season.

LOUISIANA

No special provisions for bow hunting, although the bow is recognized as a weapon. Occasional local pre-seasons have been granted. It is illegal to shoot rough fish in Louisiana. Licenses: Resident: $1. Non-Resident: four-day $5. Season: $25.

MAINE

With one of the largest deer herds in the country, Maine has given the archer several special seasons, usually of two weeks duration, before the regular gunning time. Licenses: Resident: $4.25. Non-Resident: $10.25. Maine also requires the use of a guide in the deep woods. Bows must have a minimum pull of 40 pounds and the broadheads must measure 1½" by ⅞", or larger.

MARYLAND

Has set aside special bow hunting seasons in the past for deer. Small game subject to same rules as gunning. Special deer season has allowed one deer of either sex. Licenses: Resident (county): $1.25. Resident (state): $5.25. Non-Resident: $20. Maryland allows the use of very light bows, 30 pounds being the minimum and to date no size limit has been set on broadheads.

MASSACHUSETTS

The hunting of all game is permitted with the bow and arrow, subject to normal hunting restrictions. A regulation requires that each arrow must bear the owner's name and address. No fishing is allowed with the bow. Licenses: Resident: $3.25. Non-Resident: $15.25.

MICHIGAN

Long a leader in bow hunting, Michigan has reported many violations of the game laws by bow hunters in the past few years. Under normal practice the state sets up special pre-seasons for bow hunters and allows the taking of either deer or bear, subject to local regulations. If the bow hunter does not take his game during the pre-season he can obtain a special permit to continue hunting with either a bow or a gun during the regular season. State law forbids the bow hunter to carry firearms of any sort during the pre-season and it is forbidden to carry a strung bow in a car. Bear and deer may not be taken while in the water. Archers' licenses: Resident: $3. Non-Resident: $10.

MINNESOTA

Has allowed a special deer season for bow hunters of thirty days with a bag limit of one deer of either sex. Archers are also allowed to hunt during the regular season. It is legal to shoot rough fish in Minnesota. Licenses: Resident, hunting: $3.50; bow $3.50. Non-Resident hunting: $50; bow $10.25.

MISSISSIPPI

Bow hunting is legal although fish may not be taken by this method. There have been special deer seasons for buck with horns of over 4". Licenses: Resident (county): $1.25; (state): $3.25. Non-Resident: $50.25. Small game: $25.25.

MISSOURI

Missouri has set aside a special deer season in the Ozark Mountain area for bow hunters, but this is subject to change. Gar and turtle may be taken with the bow. Licenses: Resident: $5. Non-Resident: $20. For further information write the Missouri State Game Commission, Jefferson City, Missouri.

HUNTING AND SEASONS

MONTANA
> The bow is recognized as a legal weapon in Montana, but so far there have been no special seasons, areas or concessions for the bow hunter. Licenses: Resident $5. Non-Resident: $100.

NEBRASKA
> Bow is legal but there have been no concessions to archers. Licenses: Resident: $1.50. Non-Resident: same as in home state but not less than $10.00.

NEVADA
> The bow is considered legal for the taking of all game, but no fish. There has been no special season but the game commission has, in the past, set aside an excellent reserve for bow hunters. Licenses: Resident hunting: $3.50; deer: $2.50. Non-Resident hunting: $10; deer $25.

NEW HAMPSHIRE
> Has in the past set up a special pre-season for deer. This bow hunting season has usually run for ten days and archers may also hunt during the regular season. No fish may be taken in the state with the bow. Licenses: Resident: $2.25, plus archer's tag: $2.00. Non-Resident: $20, plus $3 archer's tag.

NEW JERSEY
> Established a two week pre-season on deer for bow hunters, but this is up to the discretion of the state game commission. It is legal to take carp with a bow if the archer holds a regular state fishing license. Licenses: Resident: $3.15. Non-Resident: $15.50.

NEW MEXICO
> Recognizes the bow as a legal weapon but does not set any minimal limits on tackle. Allows one deer (buck or doe) and one bear. Has, in the past, set up a special pre-season in one area, but this is liable to change. Archers who hunt in special season may also hunt during regular season but not with guns. Fishing is legal. Licenses: Varied according to game hunted: For further information write to the Department of Fish and Game, State of New Mexico, Santa Fe, New Mexico.

NEW YORK
> Has had a special pre-season for bow hunters several years, allowing one deer and one bear. Pre-season is usually two weeks. Because of way the state is divided it is advisable to get full information from Conservation Department, The State of New York, Albany, New York. Fish may be taken in certain areas, as may frogs—but frogs require a regular hunting license—and fish, rough or otherwise, require a fishing license. Bows used for big game must be a minimum of 45 pounds. Licenses: Resident: $2.25. Non-Resident: $10.50. Bow hunters must have a special tag: $5.25.

NORTH CAROLINA
> The bow and arrow are not considered legal in this state, although there seems to be no real objection to their use. Bow hunters can, however, hunt in the Pisgah National Forest, under the supervision of the U. S. Forest Service. Licenses: Resident: $4.10. Non-Resident: $15.75.

NORTH DAKOTA
> Bow is considered illegal.

OHIO

There are no special seasons for bow hunters, and no big game hunting for anyone. Bow and arrows may be used under same conditions as guns. Game commission has in past set up bow and shot-gun seasons for deer. Licenses: Resident: $1.25. Non-Resident: $15.25.

OREGON

Has, in the past, set aside special seasons for bow hunters in specified areas. In all five of the sections the limit has been one deer of either sex. Bow hunters must have a permit to hunt, but this is furnished free with regular license. Bows used must pull at least 40 pounds and the arrows must weigh one ounce and carry a barbless broadhead not less than 7/8" wide. Further information may be had from the Information and Education Department, Oregon State Game Commission, Portland, Oregon.

PENNSYLVANIA

In 1951 the state passed a law allowing the Game Commission to establish special bow hunting seasons at its discretion. The Commission has set up such a season every year since then. In addition there are two large reserves for the exclusive use of bow hunters. The Commission may also elect to allow a doe season. Licenses: Resident: $3.15. Non-Resident: $20. Archery permit: $2. If a doe season is declared the doe license is $1.10.

RHODE ISLAND

No regulation available.

SOUTH CAROLINA

The bow is legal in South Carolina and can be used on any game. It is also legal for taking rough fish. There are no special seasons or reserves. Licenses: Resident (county): $1.10; (state): $3.10. Non-Resident: $15.25.

SOUTH DAKOTA

While the bow is considered a legal weapon there are no special seasons or reserves and the only game (protected) that can be taken by the bow are deer and pronghorn antelope. Rough fish may also be taken legally.

TENNESSEE

Bow hunting is legal. Small game regulations same as those governing gun hunting. Big game hunting with a bow is confined to the Cherokee National Park, where a special hunt is managed each year. The archer may, in this hunt take one buck, one bear and/or boar. This is the best known wild boar hunt in the country. Bows "suitable to kill big game" are required. Licenses: Resident: $2. Non-Resident: $6. Cost of Cherokee Hunt: $6.

TEXAS

Bow hunting is legal throughout most of the state, although some areas have omitted to list the bow under "legal weapons." There are no special seasons or areas, but game may be taken according to gunning laws. Permission to hunt must be obtained from land owners. Licenses: Resident: $12.15. Non-Resident: $25.

UTAH

No laws govern bow hunting but the game commission can and does establish special archery seasons for big game in certain areas. Special season is usually two weeks with a bag limit of one deer of either sex. Licenses: Resident: $4. Non-Resident: $30.

HUNTING AND SEASONS

VERMONT
Recognizes the bow as a legal weapon and has in the past held 30-day seasons in certain specified areas. Law calls for the use of bows with a minimum draw of 35 pounds and broadheads ⅞" wide, without barbs. Licenses: Resident: $2.25. Non-Resident: $15. For further information write to the State Game Commission, The State of Vermont, Montpelier, Vt.

VIRGINIA
Has in the past established special bow hunting areas for big game, including deer, bear and turkey. Small game subject to same rules and regulations as gun hunting. License: Resident: $3.50. Non-Resident: $15.75.

WASHINGTON
No special bow licenses required but archers must hold hunting licenses. The state has previously allowed bow hunters exclusive use of a 25,000 acre tract. Bow limit: 40 pounds: broadheads ⅞". Licenses: Resident: $5. Non-Resident: $25.

WEST VIRGINIA
Has set up special bow hunting seasons and areas. Bow hunting is also legal in any part of state, subject to gun regulations, during the normal hunting season. Bag limit is governed by regular game laws. It is the only state to recognize that women may use a lighter bow. Limits: Women: 35 pounds; men: 45 pounds. Arrow heads must be barbless with a minimum width of ⅞". Licenses: Resident: $2. Non-Resident: $20.

WISCONSIN
Has in the past granted a state-wide pre-season bow hunting period of 50 days, plus the right to hunt with bow during regular season. It is also legal to take fish with the bow. Licenses: Resident: $2.50; resident small game: $2. Non-Resident small game and bear: $25.

WYOMING
Archery is legal but very expensive for out-of-staters. Hunters must have special archery permit as well as hunting license. Licenses: Resident: $5. Non-Resident: $100.

ALASKA
Bow hunting has been permitted, for small game only. However, special permission has been granted to individuals in the past.

MEXICO
Archer-hunters are welcomed in Mexico. The federal authorities have been most cooperative with U. S. citizens who wish to bow hunt in our sister republic. However, since hunting is subject to state law, the archer should contact the International Hunting and Fishing Club, Mexico City, Mexico, D. F. This organization will furnish complete information and assist in planning any type of hunt.

CANADA
Ottawa states (1953) that hunting with a bow is permissible wherever gun hunting is allowed. Only restriction listed is a prohibition against hunting in the Northwest Territories. Since this area is not open to hunting by non-residents under any circumstances, it does not represent a deprivation. The Yukon section of the Northwest is open to hunting. Due to local laws, archers planning a Canadian trip should check with the proper provincial authorities.

Animal targets situated in hidden positions in the woods add to thrill of field archers, test alertness.

Practice and Games

Aside from matching the thrills of a tournament as well as the hunt, this kind of shooting makes for skill.

There are a lot of things you can do with a bow, most of which you'll want to try, sooner or later. Most of them are competitive in nature so that you can share your enjoyment, with your family or friends. To list them all would be impossible in so short a space and besides, you'll probably come up with your own variations.

Courtesy Archery Magazine

PRACTICE AND GAMES

TARGET ROUNDS

Both men and women compete in shooting rounds, although some are exclusively for men and some for women. The following rounds are those which are shot at local, state and national tournaments.

York—for men only, considered the toughest of them all. The archers shoot seventy-two arrows at one hundred yards, forty-eight at eighty and twenty-four at sixty. Scoring, as in all standard rounds, is: gold-9, red-7, blue-5, black-3, white-1. A hit on the skirt of the target does not count. An arrow which hits and bounces scores 5, as does an arrow which passes completely through the target. If an arrow cuts the line between two colors, it counts as a hit in the inner ring, subject to approval by the range captain.

Columbia—for women only. Three distances with two dozen arrows shot at each. Fifty, forty and thirty yards. In all tournament shooting the total number of arrows shot at any one distance is divisible by six—the six arrows forming one end.

Metropolitan—for men. Thirty arrows shot at each of the following distances—one hundred, eighty, sixty, fifty and forty yards.

Metropolitan—for women. Thirty arrows shot at each of the following distances—sixty, fifty, forty and thirty yards.

National—for women only. Forty-eight arrows at sixty yards and twenty-four at fifty.

American—for men and women. Thirty arrows at sixty, thirty at fifty and thirty at forty yards. Tournament shooting often includes a Multiple American, usually a total of six rounds.

Junior American—for boys only. Twenty-four arrows at

At right is another type of field target, a standard arrangement of gold bull with five color-rings.

When installing a field target course, be sure that locations are safe so arrows will not glance.

Courtesy Paul Will

Photos courtesy
Archery Magazine

Background of a hill is very safe: arrows can't fly over target and hurt people who may be strolling in fields.

It's extra good to have targets at different levels, since this trains skill in sighting fast at difficult positions.

PRACTICE AND GAMES

each of the following distances—forty, thirty and twenty yards.

All these rounds are shot by individuals for both score and hits, since the scoring lists both the total number of points and the total number of hits. In group competition there are two common team rounds.

Ohio Round—men's team shoot. Ninety-six arrows at sixty yards.

Women's Team Round—Ninety-six arrows at fifty yards.

WANDS

Among the most interesting of the novelties in archery is the wand shoot. Originally the mark was a peeled wand, stuck upright in the ground. Some archers still shoot this way. Under ordinary circumstances, however, the wand shoot is at a strip of paper pasted vertically on the target face, or at a two-inch wide strip marked down a six-foot board. Men shoot thirty-six arrows at one hundred yards and women shoot thirty-six arrows at sixty yards.

CLOUTS

Again, a very old form of archery practice, modified today. Originally the arrows were shot high in the air and the object was to drop them at a small target. Now, we use a regular target on the ground, often a flag being the only mark for aiming. The target measures forty-eight feet in diameter, with the same number of rings and same scoring—9 for gold, 7 for a red, etc. Normal tackle is used in clout shooting, although light bows may not have the necessary cast for the distance. Ordinary clout shooting calls for men to shoot thirty-six arrows at one hundred and eighty yards. Women shoot the same number of arrows at one hundred and forty or one hundred and twenty yards. A variant on clouts has been devised by the field archers, called:

BATTLE CLOUTS

The distance is increased to two hundred yards and the diameter of the target shrinks. With a diameter of twelve feet

The quick draw in roving or field archery is excellent practice for hunting later, where targets are moving.

and a bull six feet wide. Scoring is nine for center, seven, five, three and one. Broadhead arrows are used in battle clouts, with a minimum weight of one ounce and a blade at least 7/8 inch wide.

FLIGHT SHOOTING

A flight shooter is usually one of the most avid archers in the world, with little thought or regard for any phase of sport save his own. He shoots for distance and distance alone, using any means he can, to get that extra foot. Flight bows and flight arrows are a thing apart, treated by their owners like so many fine jewels. Although normal bows may be used, the addicts make and keep flight bows for the one purpose. The flight arrow is usually barreled, with the thickest part of the swell about nine or ten inches forward of the nock. The arrow must be stiff enough to be used in a very heavy bow and at the same time be as light as possible in order to get that extra yard. The vast majority of modern flight arrows are made of aluminum and are fletched with tiny plastic vanes, rather than feathers. The piles are small and the whole arrow is designed to get the arrow as far away as possible.

Flight shooting is divided into regular and free-style. In the first, the archer is required to hold the bow in his hands and draw it, unassisted. The free-style, however, allows him much more latitude. The most common version is a foot-bow, drawing up to and over two hundred pounds.

Heavy bales of hay or straw, backed with wood for support, make best base for most field targets.
Courtesy Paul Will

PRACTICE AND GAMES

The archer sits on the ground and places both feet on the belly of the bow, on either side of the grip in stirrups. Then he leans back so his feet are at an angle and draws with both hands.

The first great flight shot was made back in 1795 by a mild little Turk, who was secretary to the Turkish Ambassador to England. Using a fully reflexed, composite Turkish bow, Mahmoud Effendi shot an arrow for a distance of slightly over 480 yards. He was very modest about the feat, claiming that it was under par in his homeland, but it took many years for either Europeans or Americans to come close to the mark. It wasn't until 1939 that an American, Curtis Hill, shooting regulation style, hit a mark of 517 yards to break the record set by Mahmoud Effendi. Apparently the free-style shooters' longest mark, although an unofficial one, is seven hundred and fifty-eight yards and one foot. It was shot in California at a state meet, using a bow that drew two hundred and ten pounds.

ARCHERY GOLF

Currently one of the most popular forms of archery, archery golf is unfortunately confined mostly to the Midwest and West. The NFAA reports that there are no courses where it is officially played on the Eastern Seaboard. It is extremely popular in the West and Northwest where special equipment is used. The usual tackle calls for a flight bow and three arrows—one

Courtesy Archery Magazine

At right is twin-target shooting: men draw at same time. Small river is equivalent to "sand trap."

Some enthusiastic field archers even shoot at night, although this is extreme test of skill, eye.

Courtesy Paul Will

Photo of Christine Will
Courtesy Paul Will

Field archery is favorite of women also, who participate in all kinds of weather. Note marker.

Husband-wife teams are popular: here, Bill and Marion Dasch didn't do too well at 50-yard range.

Courtesy Archery Magazine

PRACTICE AND GAMES

flight, one approach and one putting. The archer can only use the one bow, but he can change arrows as often as desired. In other areas the archers are required to use only normal tackle.

Played on a standard golf course the object is to go around in the lowest number of shots. Drive, approach and putt are all the same as in actual golf. The only concession is that instead of driving the arrow into the cup the archer shoots at a small soft ball or disc which is placed just off the ground immediately beside the cup. An arrow less than its own length from the mark is conceded as "in." Played in active competition with golfers, the archers often have to give a handicap. Nine under par is usually the average for a nine-hole course. The game is so popular because it is one in which everyone can compete without any distinction and also it is easy enough for the beginner to get a decent score his first or second time out. A good score for nine holes is between thirty and thirty-three but it has been done in less.

POPINJAY SHOOTING

This is an import from France and Belgium. Although it is little practiced in this country it deserves mention, not only for its tradition but for its picturesqueness. A tall mast or pole is erected and at various intervals along its length, cross members are fastened. At the ends of these cross bars, cloth or cardboard birds are placed and the archers, standing on measured distance marks, attempt to knock the "birds" off their roosts.

These archers are practicing with bird- or small game-arrows: note extra large feathers and blunt heads.

Approximating conditions of a real hunt, girls have sighted target and take aim immediately.

PRACTICE AND GAMES

FIELD ROUNDS

There are even more possible field rounds than there are target rounds. Although field archery, as such, is new, its practitioners are an ardent lot, constantly evolving new ways of testing their skill. The basic shooting of the field archer is a variation of the old game of rovers, called the **Roving Field Round**. It involves either fourteen or twenty-eight targets shot at varying distances and from different positions. In the case of a fourteen-target round, the archers repeat the shooting to bring their total to twenty-eight. Four target faces are used—twenty-four-inch, with a twelve-inch center and a spot of four inches; eighteen-inch face with a center of nine inches and a three-inch spot; a foot-wide face with a six-inch center and a spot of two inches and a six-inch face with a three-inch center and a one-inch spot. Some faces are ringed in black with the center white and the spot black, while others are animal targets, with the round faces superimposed. A hit anywhere in the circle, including the spot is counted for five and anywhere else on the actual face area scores three. Bounces and penetrations are scored as three points, if witnessed. An arrow counts for the higher score when it cuts the ring dividing the two areas.

In actual shooting at the targets, in a unit of fourteen, the following arrows must be shot:

Fifteen, twenty, twenty-five and thirty yards at one of the 12-inch faces (four arrows at each of the above distances);

Forty, forty-five and fifty yards at one of the 18-inch faces (four arrows at each of the above distances);

Fifty-five, sixty and sixty-five yards at one of the 24-inch faces (four arrows at each of the above distances);

Four four-position targets are also included. In these each arrow is shot at the same distance, but from a different position or at a different target.

Thirty-five yards at an 18-inch target face;

Thirty, thirty-five, forty and forty-five yards at an 18-inch target face;

Fifty, sixty, seventy and eighty yards at a 24-inch target face;

Twenty, twenty-five, thirty and thirty-five feet at a 6-inch target face.

With a combination of targets, such as this round gives you, over rough terrain and often in thick brush, it's easy to see why the field archer changes into a hunter with no strain. The whole layout is designed to give the archer a complete command of his weapon under any and all circumstances.

Field archery also lists a round shot with broadheads, on a course similar to the **Roving Field Round,** a round where the archer who scores must step back one pace from the normal mark for each score he makes. There are dozens of others; like the basic round all are designed to sharpen the archer's ability, without subjecting him to the nervous strain which is often felt in tournaments among target archers.

HORSEBACK ARCHERY

Fairly new as a competitive sport, horseback archery is perhaps the most difficult of all, since it requires not only fine bowmanship, but a very good seat aboard a horse. Targets, or butts are placed in various spots around a big open area and the archers, one at a time, ride full tilt past the butts, trying to put their arrows in the marks. Long bows are almost totally useless in this sport because of their length and the ideal bow is either an extremely short flat-bow or a short recurve. The sport had its obvious origin among the American Indians who hunted buffalo with a bow on horseback. To date, **Horseback Archery** is disorganized, requiring as it does the combination of skills, the big space and the horses. However, in the Southwest, many archers are practicing it as a means of preparation for horseback hunting. While the buffalo is gone as a hunter's quarry, there are still a lot of javelina or peccaries in some of the desert states and bow hunting for them from horseback may prove to be one of the most exciting archery sports to be evolved in this country. Certainly if the horseback archer finds a closed season on javelina he can always try his hand at jack rabbits from the back of an intelligent cow pony.

BOW FISHING

This is the archer's year-round delight, the hunting of fish, large and small, with archery tackle. From Minnesota to Florida, from Maine to California, archers find fish to provide sport and food, at almost any time of the year. Because many of the fish hunted are rough or coarse, like the gars and carp, the bow hunter serves a double barreled purpose. Not only does he get a lot of fun out of the hunt, but he acts as the agent of conservation authorities, to whom the rough fish are usually anathema.

Markers are placed along field route to indicate where archer must stand to shoot proper distance.

Varying shooting position of field participants adds interest, also approximates hunt-conditions.

Auxiliary equipment for this type of hunting is simple and inexpensive. Actually all you really need are some fish heads, for your arrows. There are many variations on the fish head but basically it follows a single principle—a design calling for a head making a small hole on entering the target and expanding, preventing withdrawal. Some of the heads use a single long barb, set on a hinged point—when the line tightens, the head turns crosswise in the target. Others feature a spring barb which releases itself when it enters flesh. Some archers, after really giant fish, use extremely wide broadheads, with a hole bored through one of the barbs, to hold the line. Here, pressure on the line turns the head sideways and makes withdrawal difficult. A reel, to hold your line is also needed in this type of hunting. Some hunters, working from boats, use reels that are attached to ordinary fishpoles. Line is payed out and laid so that it will run free and then attached to the fish head. After a hit is made, the archer puts down his bow and plays the fish from the rod. If however, you're after smaller fish and working in the water yourself, a reel fastened to the bow is what you'll need. Such reels are manufactured by most of the tackle makers and are placed on the bow by means of set screws, so that they are not permanent. You yourself can make a simple reel by fixing a short length of auto radiator hose to the back of the bow with C-clamps. The fishing line is wound around the hose, which points in the direction of the arrow. When the arrow flies the line is fastened directly to the bow and the archer then plays his fish by hand.

HIAWATHA SHOOTING

When Longfellow wrote that his Indian hero Hiawatha shot several arrows in the air at one time, he probably didn't think that he was starting an archery trick. Since that time, almost every archer, has at one time or another, tried to duplicate and beat Hiawatha's record. An old manuscript on Arab Archery states that some of the Oriental bowmen could put sixteen arrows up at once. No one has, to date, equalled this mark but it's fairly easy to equal the Hiawatha score.

Be sure that you are working in open country and that no one is walking in or around the danger zone. While Hiawatha shooting is a lot of fun, it violates one of the cardinal rules of archery safety.

Hold the arrows to be shot in your bow hand and keep practicing. If you are making your own arrows, you might cut double nocks in a group. Set the two at right angles to one another so that in actual practice you don't have to waste time in nocking. Remember that, as in flight shooting, there is no established form—just get your arrows up in the air. •

PRACTICE AND GAMES

Photo by Mark Swain
Courtesy Archery Magazine

Field tours are held in all kinds of terrain: here, Hazel Rich holds bead on target in California desert.

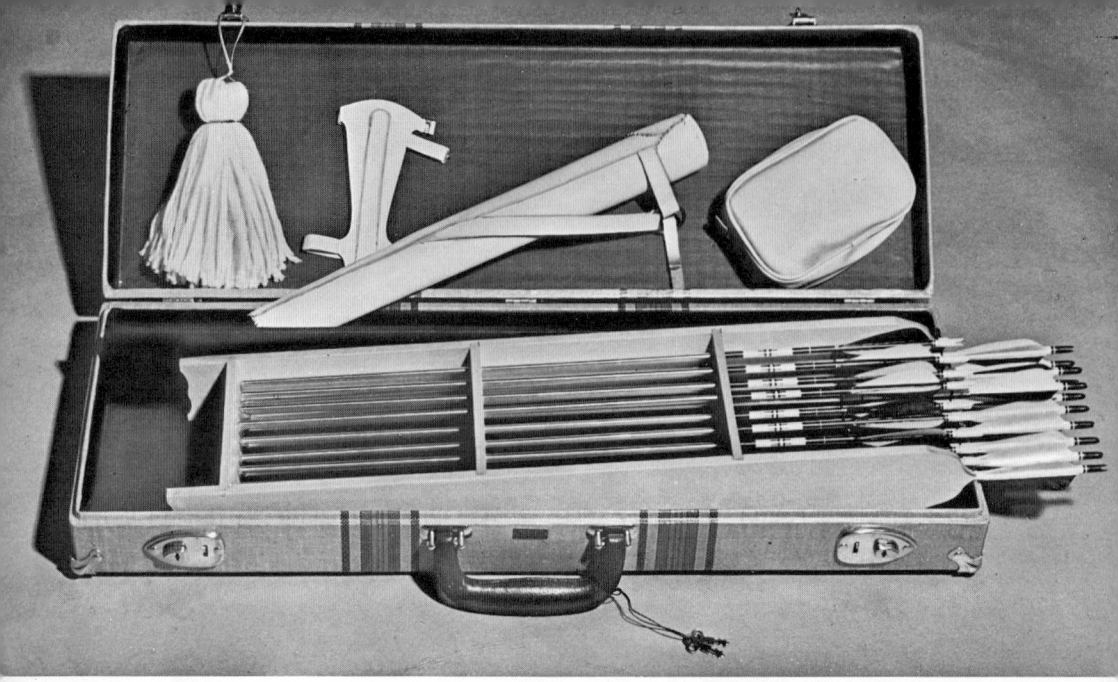

Arrow rack shown above in carrying case helps keep arrows from warping. The case-top contains, left to right, tassel, an arm guard, quiver, gadget bag.

Accessories

The most important accesories to an archer are finger tabs and arm guards, but there are a dozen other useful pieces as well.

FIRST and foremost among accessories are those designed for finger protection. Even a light bow can make your fingers very sore after a day's shooting and with a hunting bow it's easy to draw blood from those three vital finger tips. Of the two main types of finger protection, the tab is the simplest, both to use and to make. The tab is cut from soft but thick leather, usually with a razor blade or scissors (see shapes in photo top of page 135). The two-finger tab is more commonly used, although some champion archers feel that the one-finger version permits of greater accuracy.

Another, and even simpler form of finger protection is an old, soft glove. If you are using a heavy bow, sew small tabs of heavier leather onto the tips of the three glove fingers that hold the string.

Some people prefer open cots (see patterns at lower left of page 135), which slide over the fingers and are not anchored in any way. They are quite useful, but show a tendency to brush off or drop in rough terrain and in wooded areas.

It's a good plan to soak the cots thoroughly, after you've sewn them, and then place them on your finger tips to dry. The leather will take on the proper shape that way and help to keep them from falling off.

To be doubly sure, attach strips of leather or tough elastic to the tops of the cots and run them back to a snap-buttoned cuff at your wrist. The end result is a muchly cut out glove, that will protect

Accessories

Arm Guards and Finger Tabs

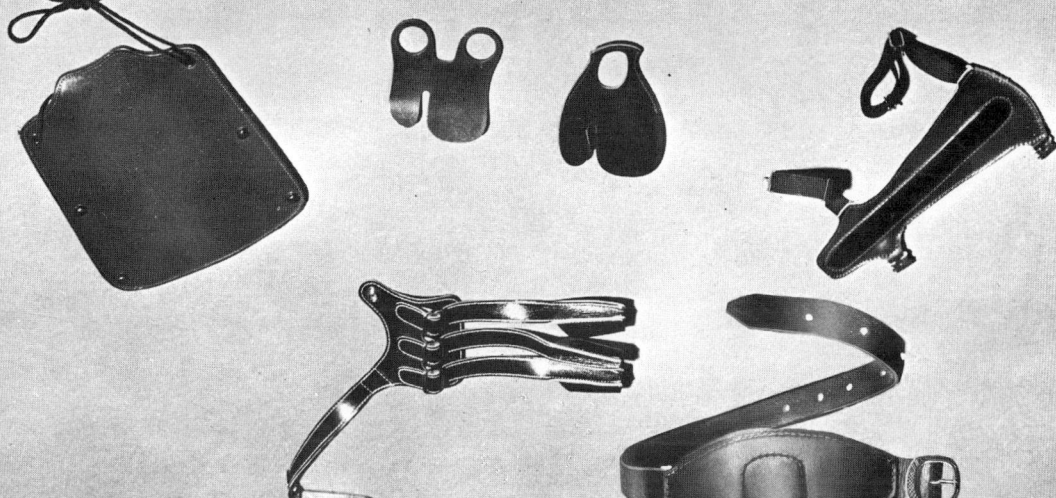

Photo by Hal Kelly

From left to right above are shown arm guard, two- and one-finger tabs, cots, another guard style.

At right is close-up of one kind of arm guard, a commercial model, showing reinforced center.

Below are patterns for cots: cut out of a hard leather, soak and shape to fingers after sewing.

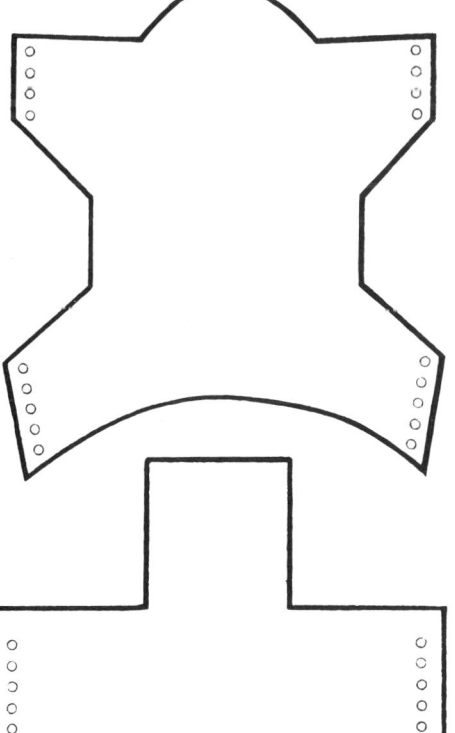

Good homemade finger protection: cut away an old glove, sew tabs at finger ends. Result is below.

135

Quivers

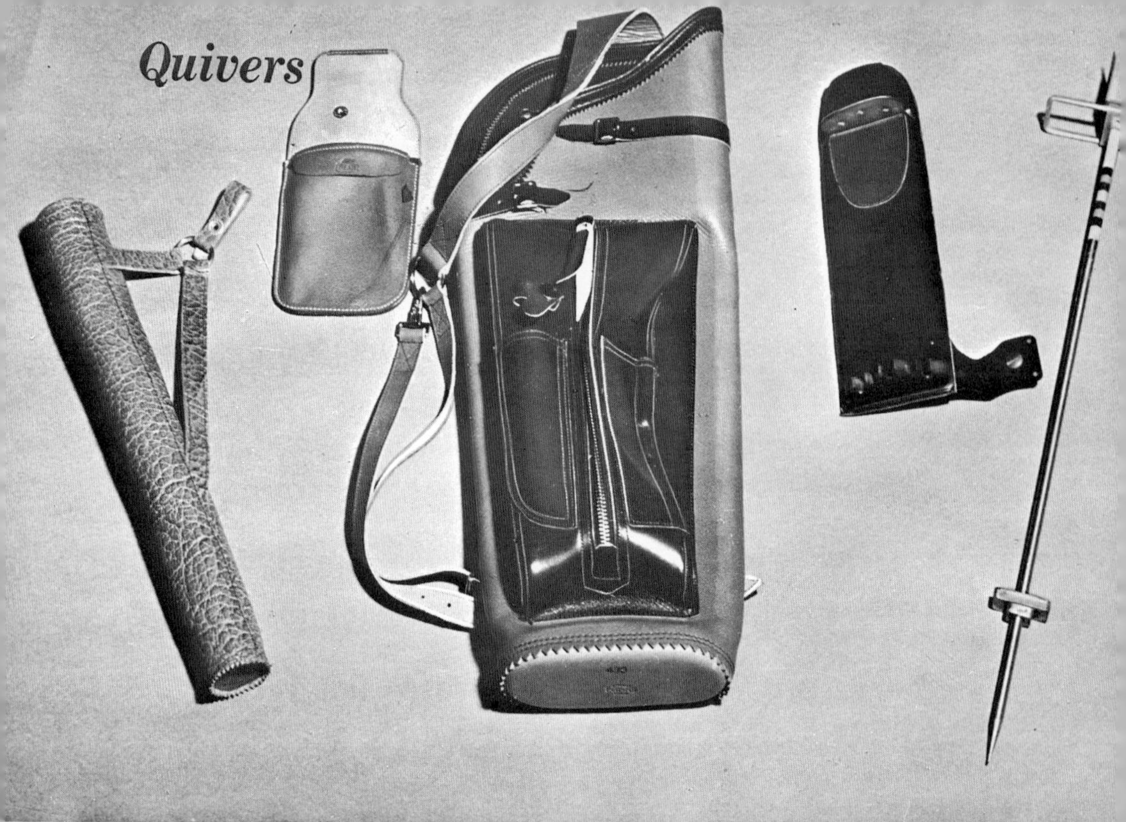

Photo by Hal Kelly

Quiver types, left to right, are: belt, pocket, shoulder (for hunting or field), target and, finally, ground quiver.

Close-up of typical hunting quiver: it has a zippered pocket for carrying few extra supplies.

Medium-size quiver shown below can be used for all purposes: hunting, roving, field or target.

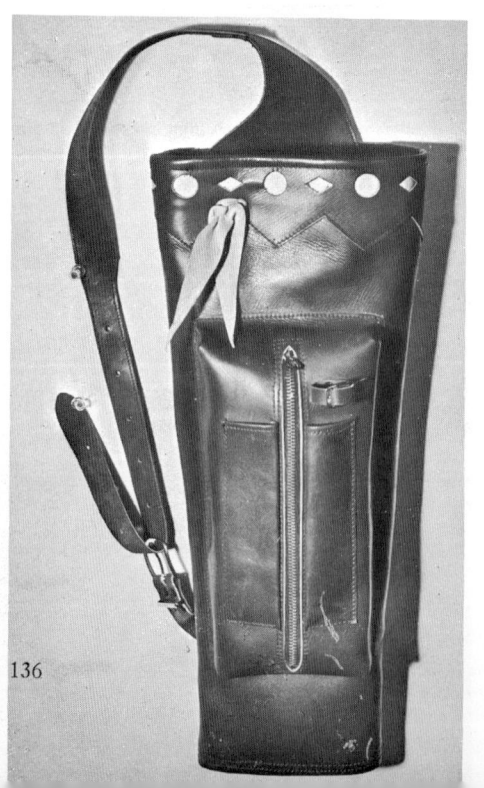

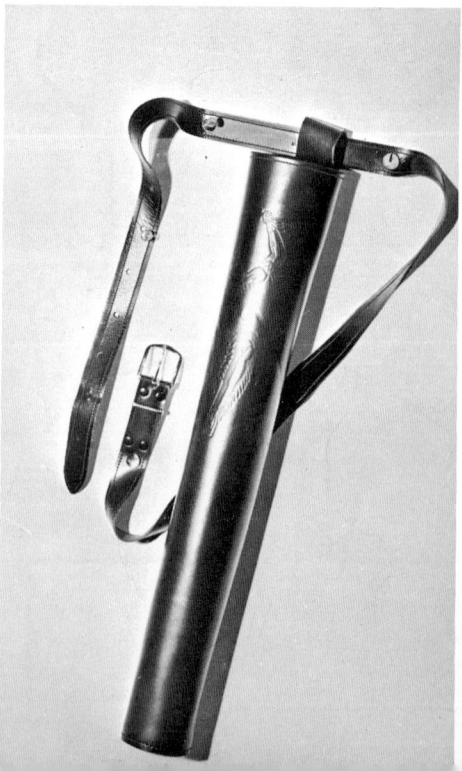

ACCESSORIES

Arrow Points

your fingers, without covering the hand.

The bracer or arm guard is next on the program. If you've ever heard anyone say a bracer is unnecessary, that person didn't know what he or she was talking about. Too many competent archers wear them, for them to be superfluous. The bracer not only protects the bow-arm of the shooter but also gives the bow string a flat, even surface against which to strike, which in turn sends the arrow on its way without deflection. Even if the string, striking your arm, doesn't hurt you, it will catch momentarily, either on the skin or on your sleeve and your aim will suffer.

Almost any smooth surface, on the inside of the bow arm from wrist up will do the trick. The only thing to watch out for is that the guard comes far enough up the arm so the string will not catch behind it. Leather has been the traditional material for bracers, either laced or buckled, but lately many of the commercial bracers are made of lucite. In an emergency you can bind a long pencil to your wrist with a pair of rubber bands—not as a permanent job, of course, but only to take the strain of an afternoon's shooting, if you should forget to bring along your regular arm guard.

Another bit of equipment, particularly for field or hunting, is the arrow tassel. It isn't absolutely necessary, but is a bright, picturesque addition to the archer's costume. Fine soft wool, of a bright color, is the best material to use, although some archers like to make their tassels of soft leather strands, such as chamois, or old suede. In either case the tassel is easy to make.

Take a leather thong, approximately six inches long and tie a coarse knot in one end. Then, tie your wool to the thong, securing it just above the knot with the free ends toward the other end of the thong. When you have the tassel built up, reverse the strands of wool, so that they fall around the knot on the leather thong. Tie in place, below the thong knot, this time using several lengths of contrastingly colored wool. If the lengths of yarn are uneven, trim them with a pair of scissors—and your tassel is complete. The free end of the thong can be attached to belt or quiver.

The quiver is again a matter of personal taste. There are several kinds, but they are largely limited to use in the type of archery for which they were designed. In target work there are belt quivers, pocket quivers and ground quivers. For field work,

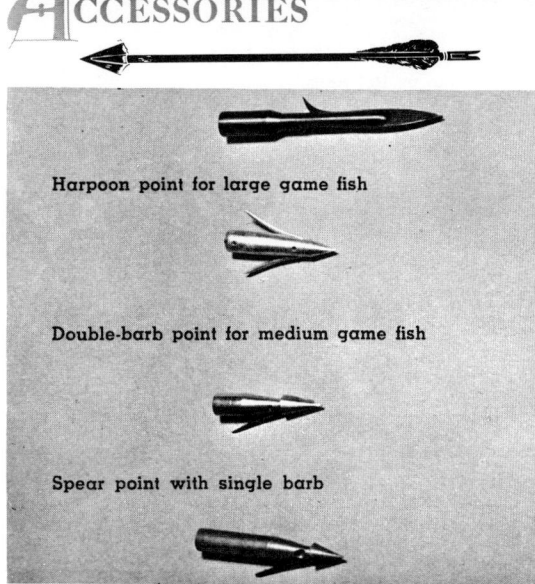

Harpoon point for large game fish

Double-barb point for medium game fish

Spear point with single barb

Photos by Hal Kelly

Larger spear point for bow fishing

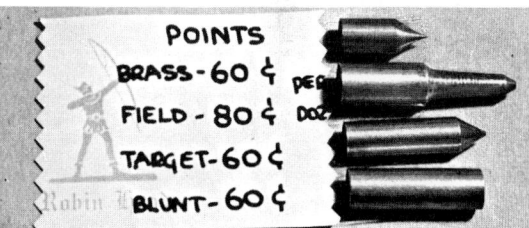

Points shown above are used for various kinds of competition, with exception of blunt point, used for bird hunting. Below is an array of broadheads, styles used for big and medium-size game hunting.

Photo by Hal Kelly

Bowsights

Aiming in archery is tricky: sighting is not done along arrow point, as most people believe, but on target itself. Eyes act as rear sight always, so a front sight on bow is big accuracy aid.

and hunting, you have the back quiver and the belt type.

The ground quiver is simply made but is useless for an archer who is moving. It is placed in the ground at the shooting line, when you're shooting at targets. The bow is often left across it when you go to the target to collect the arrows. It is a piece of stiff wire, with a horizontal loop in one end about five inches in diameter. The straight end is stuck in the ground, by the shooting line and the arrows are dropped through the loop on top.

The pocket quiver is a flap of stiff leather, inserted, fold down, in the hip pocket. Target archers, shooting three arrows at an end, often find it convenient to use this very simple quiver. Others omit the quiver and simply put the arrows, pile down, into their pockets, where they are easily reached.

The belt quiver is tubular, straight and simple. True to its name it hangs from the belt and is used both in target archery and in the field or in hunting. Usually of soft leather, it can be made of heavy cloth, with metal loops to give it roundness. A mailing tube, of sufficient width, cut to length, with the bottom padded and the sides decorated will make quite an acceptable belt quiver that should wear well.

One form of quiver, the flat or Indian style, can be worn either at the belt or across the back. A large piece of leather, preferably horsehide, is used. It should be ten inches wide and twenty inches long. Fold it double and stitch down the long side and one end. The resulting flat sheath is twenty inches deep and five wide. At the bottom be sure that your stitches are double, since arrows will sometimes work through otherwise. You might add a doubled strip of felt along the inside of this area before it is sewn, as an added precaution. The whole can then be fastened by a short strap to your belt, or flung across your shoulder by a regular belt, cut in half and the cut ends sewn onto the quiver, so that the buckle is in front where it is easily reached for adjustment.

The big over-the-shoulder quiver is the last of the main types. For the hunting archer the quiver is a constant companion, like his bow. Most hunters decorate their quivers with pockets and straps, to carry extra supplies. But no matter what the form and style, always remember that the quiver must be silent. When you are hunting—and it's also a good idea to think this way in field work—silence is essential. The

Accessories

At left is bowsight in action: archer after experimenting adjusts it to suit his particular eye level.

Close-up of one kind of bowsight, showing way it is attached to bow: other types vary in attachment.

The King bowsight, below, has movable carriage and can be set to show bow elevation, wind drift.

scrape of a small branch across stiff leather or canvas causes your game to flee, before you even see it. For this very reason many archers set up a system of leather webbing inside the quiver itself so that the shafts, in moving, will not rattle against each other.

To make a good, sturdy, adequate quiver use a heavy leather. Oil-tanned horsehide is excellent. Laid out, it should be in the form of a rough quadrilateral—the long sides twenty inches deep, the top, twelve inches wide and the bottom, nine. The bottom, also of horsehide, should be cut in the form of an oval, or a circle—whichever form you prefer for the finished quiver. Form your big piece into a tube and scribe the dimension of the lower end, to cut out the bottom.

Next lay the quiver body flat and with dividers mark a series of points along the two long sides. These points should be spaced a quarter of an inch in from the edge and about a quarter of an inch apart. Then mark more points along the nine-inch edge, measured the same way. The bottom should now be marked, taking care that the marks on the bottom correspond to those you've made along the nine-inch edge of the body.

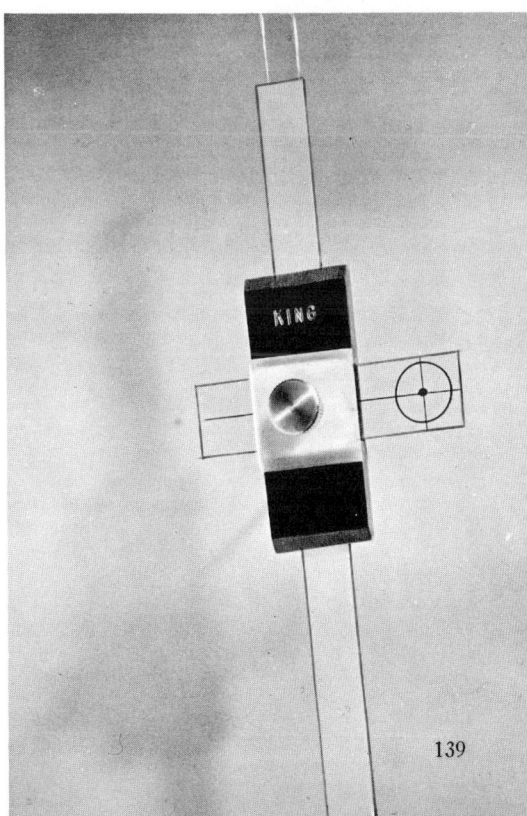

Courtesy King Co.

Courtesy American Archery Co.

Miscellaneous Accessories

At left is shown handle-section of aluminum bow. New, it is unaffected by temperature as other bows.

Stringserver below replaces worn-out servings in few minutes. Tool is turned around bowstring.

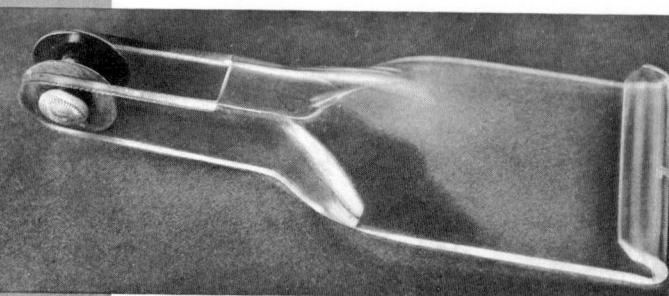

Courtesy Master Co.

A good leather punch is needed now. It is possible to use hot wire and burn holes where you've marked, but this is a long, slow, smelly job. For a much faster and neater job, punch out your holes on the indicated points.

Next take your bottom piece and glue a pad of sponge rubber on its top, keeping the diameter of the rubber cushion such that the whole thing will fit up into the quiver, when you come to lace it. On top of the rubber, glue two layers of good sturdy felt. This may sound complicated, but it will not only lessen noise, it will also help to keep your broadheads good and sharp.

When the padding is well set, take a strip of leather and begin to lace. Leave yourself plenty of excess and at one end of the lace tie a simple knot. Start at the inside, pull the long thong through the bottom hole of one of the sides, then through the corresponding hole in the bottom piece and back up into the next hole at the lower end of the side. Continue the process until you have the whole bottom in place. Next, take a spike and using your thumb to push it into the holes, tighten the lacing all the way. Untie the knot you left in the far end of the thong and make the two ends fast by splicing or knotting them together.

Lacing the sides is simple and you can use either a cross-stitch lacing or an overcast. If you don't want to tie it off at the

Accessories

Regulation target matte shown here is made of marsh grass and has a reinforced center to prevent wear from the constant striking.

Courtesy Saunders Archery Target Co.

top, leave enough thong so the end can be worked back down into the lacing to anchor it. This way, nothing will hinder the arrows.

To fasten the finished quiver to your shoulders, take an ordinary belt and cut it in half. The two cut ends should be machine stitched to the quiver, one at the top and one at the bottom. The actual placing of the belt ends will be governed by your own build and your own preference for quiver position, when shooting.

One last bit of equipment, and we'll be ready to get out and at it. When you're out shooting, it's a good thing to have a few essentials with you—extra bowstrings, wax, a knife, a file for sharpening broadheads, perhaps even a rabbit's foot. Belt ammunition cases purchasable at Army and Navy stores are good. But if you want to make a gadget case, here's how! Take a piece of leather—in this instance, rawhide is fine, although split cowhide is equally useful—twenty-four inches by seven. Fold so that you have a flap of five inches hanging in front. The pouch itself should be approximately nine inches deep. Sew the edges, but before you do, cut two slits in the back of the pouch, two and one half inches apart. When you put the pouch on, simply thread your belt through the two slits. Fastening for the pouch lid or flap is up to you, but with a simple pouch a simple tie of rawhide is both useful and in keeping with the whole idea. •

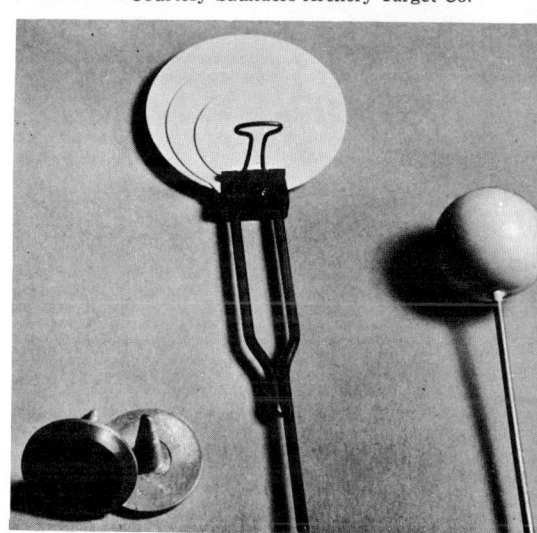

Photo by Hal Kelly

Foot markers, left, are used to establish the firing position. Point-of-aim markers, right, are set in ground somewhere in front of target to guide archer's sighting and arrow-trajectory. Below shows target line with two kinds of foot markers set alongside. These are popular for tournaments.

GLOSSARY OF TERMS

ANCHOR POINT . The point on the archer's face, to which the bow string is drawn on every shot.
ARCHERY GOLF . An adaptation of the game of golf to the sport of archery. Players shoot for the holes and score according to their accuracy. Most archery golf is played in the west and mid-west.
ARM GUARD . . . Any device which protects the archer's bow arm from the slap of the bowstring. Usually of leather, it is often called a 'bracer'.
ARROW PLATE . . A piece of material, either hard or soft, which is inset into the bow at the point where the arrow traverses the wood. In target bows the arrow plate is hard, in hunting and field bows, it is soft, to deaden the noise.
ARROW REST . . A small projection at the top of the bow handle. The arrow rests thereon during the draw. Formerly used mostly on flight bows, it is now a part of most good bows.
BACK . . . . The side of the bow which is always away from the string.
BACKED BOW . . A bow, whose back and belly are of different composition. Most backing today is in the form of specially developed plastics, or in the form of fibre glass.
BELLY . . . . . . The side of the bow which is always away from the string.
BILLETS . . . . . Short lengths of wood, which are spliced together to form a complete bow.
BOW STAVE . . . A full length piece of wood from which the bow is fashioned.
BOWYER . . . . . A bow maker.
BUTT . . . . A target built of bales of hay or straw.
CAST . . . . A term used to describe the distance over which a bow will drive an arrow.
CLOUT . . . . . . A wand at which archers shoot over a distance of 180 yards..
COCK . . . . . . More properly, cock feather, the feather which is at right angles to the bow during the draw.
COMPOSITE . . . A bow made up of more than one substance.
CREEP . . . . . . One of the major faults of the beginning archer, allowing the arrow to slide forward on the bow hand just prior to the release.
END . . . . In the U. S., six arrows shot consecutively in a target round.
EYE . . . . A name sometimes given to the loops at the end of the bowstring.
FIELD ARROW . . A heavy duty arrow designed to give maximum service in field archery without loss of accuracy.
FINGER STALL . . Tips or stalls worn on the tips of the drawing fingers to protect the flesh from chafing by the bowstring.
FISTMELE . . . . . Today, six inches. Formerly, the distance between the bow and the string when the bow is strung, measured by placing the fist on the bow handle and raising the thumb toward the string.
FLETCH . . . . . . To put the feathers on the arrow.
FLIGHT BOW . . . A bow designed for maximum cast without too much thought for accuracy.
FOLLOW . . . . . A tendency of some bows and bow woods to take for their permanent form, their strung shape.
FOOT . . . . A piece of hardwood, spliced into the arrow to give it strength.
HANDLE . . . . . The center portion of the bow, rigid and deep.
HEAD . . . . The point or pile of the arrow.
HEN FEATHERS . . The two opposing feathers to the cock.
HIGH STRUNG . . When the string is more than six inches from the bow.
HIT . . . . A score, or when the arrow strikes the target.
HOLDING . . . . . The practice of staying at full draw for a short period before the release.
LAMINATED . . . A composite bow, but usually one made of only wood.
LIMB . . . . Either the upper or lower half of the bow.
LONGBOW . . . . A bow held in the hand, by common definition, as opposed to crossbows, but more properly a specific design of bow (see text).
LOOSE . . . . . . The actual release of the drawn bow string, one of the most important parts of any style of archery.
NOCK . . . . . . Either that part of the arrow which is fitted to the string or the two ends of the bow itself where the bowstring is fitted.
NOCK POINT . . That point on the string where the arrow is nocked at all times. Often marked by extra serving.
OVERBOW . . . . To draw a bow too heavy for the individual archer.
OVERDRAW . . . . To draw the bow past the limit set for it by the bowyer. The cardinal sin of archery.
PETTICOAT . . . . The area of the target face outside of the white ring.
PILE . . . . The head of the arrow.
PIN . . . . In yew, a tiny knot in the wood of the bow stave.
POINT BLANK . . Shooting from a spot where the point of aim and the center of the target are coincidental.
POINT OF AIM . . An aid in target shooting, to establish the flight path of the arrow so as to intercept the target at center.
QUARTERING . . . Spoken of in connection with the wind, when it blows across the path of the arrow.
QUIVER . . . . . A receptacle for carrying or holding arrows.
RANGE . . . . . . The distance to be shot.
RANGE FINDER . A device used to determine the location of a point of aim.
REFLEXED BOW . Any bow whose limbs spring toward the back when it is unstrung.
ROUND . . . . . . A series of arrows, shot at a pre-fixed distance.
ROVING . . . . . A game played in which the archer-players select random targets and shoot a predetermined number of arrows at them in turn. The targets are usually selected by the winner of the previous target.
SELF . . . . A self bow is any bow made of only one substance, i.e. yew. A self arrow is unfooted.
SERVING . . . . . Extra protection for the bow string, applied where the string contacts the bow nocks and also where the arrow is nocked in shooting.
SHAFT . . . . . . The main body of the arrow.
SHOOTING LINE . In target archery the line which the shooters straddle when addressing the target.
SIGHT . . . . . . Aiming. Or an auxiliary device, fixed to the bow which enables the archer to improve his shooting.
SPINE . . . . A term used in archery to describe the flexibility, elasticity and stiffness of an arrow shaft in relation to its thickness and weight.
TAB . . . . A flat piece of leather used on the hand to protect the fingers of the archer.
TACKLE . . . . . . General term to describe any or all of an archer's gear.
TILLER . . . . . . A stick used to hold a bow at the draw while it is being made.
TIMBER HITCH . . A knot which is used at the lower end of an adjustable bow string, also called the bowyer's knot.
TOXOPHILITE . . An archer, but more particularly one who is interested in the history of the subject.
TRAJECTORY . . . The path of the arrow in flight.
VANE . . . . The feather on an arrow.
WAND . . . . . . A mark used in a form of shooting. Specifically it is two inches wide and six feet long. It is shot at from a distance of 100 yards.
WEIGHT . . . . . In describing the bow, the number of pounds of pull necessary to bring the arrow to full draw with the bow.